Mark Green has specialised in employment and discrimination law for the past 20 years. He enjoys a busy practice and appears regularly in both the employment tribunal and the Employment Appeal Tribunal for both claimants and respondents. Appointed to the Attorney-General's A Panel in 2023, he frequently represents government departments in complex matters and has a niche practice in the crossover between national security and employment law. Following the high profile age discrimination case of Jolly v Royal Berkshire NHS Foundation Trust 3324869/2017, Mark made several appearances on television, radio and in national newspapers, including discussing the case on the This Morning sofa. Mark loves to travel and speaks several languages fluently.

Karen Moss is a specialist employment barrister practicing at 3PB Barristers in London where she leads the Employment and Discrimination Group. She is frequently instructed in complcx statutory claims in employment tribunals and the Employment Appeal Tribunal, and employment-related claims in the High Court and county courts. She has extensive experience in dealing with age discrimination claims in particular. Her notable cases include acting as lead counsel representing over 50 senior cabin crew in a group action against an international airline relating to a mass redundancy exercise which was found to be unfair. Karen is ranked as Band 1 in Employment by Chambers and Partners, and as a Tier 1 Leading Junior in Employment in Legal 500 in the South Eastern region. She lives in London with her husband, and two teenaged children who frequently remind her of her comparatively great age.

Rosa Thomas was called to the bar in 2023 and practices in employment and education, specialising in equality and discrimination law. Rosa appears frequently in the employment tribunal, often in matters concerning age discrimination. Most recently, Rosa has worked on multiple cases concerning claimants with menopause and the intersection of age, sex, and disability discrimination. Prior to coming to the bar Rosa worked in public affairs at the national charity Age UK.

A Practical Guide to Age Discrimination in the Workplace

A Practical Guide to Age Discrimination in the Workplace

Mark Green, 3PB Barristers
Karen Moss, 3PB Barristers
Rosa Thomas, Garden Court Chambers

Law Brief Publishing

Published 2026 by Law Brief Publishing, an imprint of Law Brief Publishing Ltd
30 The Parks
Minehead
Somerset
TA24 8BT

www.lawbriefpublishing.com

Paperback: 978-1-916698-01-7

PREFACE

The genesis of this book came from one of the authors' experience in the case of ***Jolly v Royal Berkshire NHS Foundation Trust*** ET Case No. 3324869/2017. This was a case in which an 86 year-old NHS secretary was discriminated against and harassed because of her age and disability. Despite an excellent sickness absence record, managers made decisions about her future and ultimately dismissed her due to stereotypical assumptions about her frailty and inability to retrain. As the oldest age discrimination claimant recorded, the case received much media attention and opened up discussions about the importance of not making assumptions about age in relation to capability. We hope that this book will continue to promote such conversations.

The authors' knowledge of age discrimination claims comes from our wide-ranging expertise as barristers specialising in employment law. Between us, we have extensive experience of all forms of age discrimination claims, acted for many high-profile claimants and respondents, and developed an understanding of the legal, practical and human dimensions of age discrimination in the workplace.

Each of the authors have been inspired in writing this book by the clients they have represented in age discrimination claims, and pay tribute to the tenacity shown by many parties in their pursuit of justice. We hope that this book serves to assist parties to navigate the tribunal process more confidently.

We are very grateful to our wonderful friends and colleagues at 3PB Barristers. Our clerks, especially the brilliant Russell Porter, Patrick Robson, Patrick Steptoe and Mattie Scanlan, managed to enable us to have sufficient time away from our clients to ensure this book was written – thank you for all your hard work.

Our sincere thanks must also go to our beloved partners and families to whom this book is dedicated, especially Victor, Margaret, Marcus, Jackson, Milo, Ginny, Jonathan, Ali, Tarini, Toby and Grumpy whose unwavering support throughout this process has been much appreciated.

This book presents the law as understood at 19th May 2025. The content is not intended to provide individual case-specific advice. No liability is accepted for any reliance on the contents of this book.

Mark Green
Karen Moss
Rosa Thomas
May 2025

PREFACE

The genesis of this book came from one of the authors' experience in the case of ***Jolly v Royal Berkshire NHS Foundation Trust*** ET Case No. 3324869/2017. This was a case in which an 86 year-old NHS secretary was discriminated against and harassed because of her age and disability. Despite an excellent sickness absence record, managers made decisions about her future and ultimately dismissed her due to stereotypical assumptions about her frailty and inability to retrain. As the oldest age discrimination claimant recorded, the case received much media attention and opened up discussions about the importance of not making assumptions about age in relation to capability. We hope that this book will continue to promote such conversations.

The authors' knowledge of age discrimination claims comes from our wide-ranging expertise as barristers specialising in employment law. Between us, we have extensive experience of all forms of age discrimination claims, acted for many high-profile claimants and respondents, and developed an understanding of the legal, practical and human dimensions of age discrimination in the workplace.

Each of the authors have been inspired in writing this book by the clients they have represented in age discrimination claims, and pay tribute to the tenacity shown by many parties in their pursuit of justice. We hope that this book serves to assist parties to navigate the tribunal process more confidently.

We are very grateful to our wonderful friends and colleagues at 3PB Barristers. Our clerks, especially the brilliant Russell Porter, Patrick Robson, Patrick Steptoe and Mattie Scanlan, managed to enable us to have sufficient time away from our clients to ensure this book was written – thank you for all your hard work.

Our sincere thanks must also go to our beloved partners and families to whom this book is dedicated, especially Victor, Margaret, Marcus, Jackson, Milo, Ginny, Jonathan, Ali, Tarini, Toby and Grumpy whose unwavering support throughout this process has been much appreciated.

This book presents the law as understood at 19th May 2025. The content is not intended to provide individual case-specific advice. No liability is accepted for any reliance on the contents of this book.

Mark Green
Karen Moss
Rosa Thomas
May 2025

CONTENTS

TABLE OF CASES

TABLE OF LEGISLATION

CHAPTER ONE

INTRODUCTION

The aim of this book is to provide a step-by-step guide to all aspects of claims of age discrimination at work. It is designed to be of assistance not only for employment practitioners, but for practitioners in other areas and litigants in person alike. As this is a practical guide, we have deliberately not focussed on detailed history and jurisprudence except where necessary and useful. Wherever possible when describing various concepts, we have used examples relating specifically to age rather than other protected characteristics. These may come from our own experience, from the helpful online database of employment tribunal judgments and of course from appellate cases.

Age as a protected characteristic

'*Age is different*' held the Supreme Court when comparing it to other protected characteristics in ***Seldon v Clarkson Wright and Jakes (and Secretary of State for Business Innovation and Skills, and Age UK – Intervenors)*** [2012] UKSC 16, [2012] IRLR 590. Age is, Lady Hale held, a continuum which changes over time and is not binary in nature. As such, it is unusual amongst protected characteristics in that those who at one point in their lives may benefit from privilege or suffer discrimination as a young person will likely go on to benefit or suffer as an older person.

Age is perhaps the protected characteristic that is taken the least seriously of all nine protected characteristics under the Equality Act 2010 ('EqA'). In 2018, a survey by the Equality and Human Rights Commission ('EHRC'), revealed that 54% of the 2800 people surveyed thought that age discrimination was 'not at all' or 'only slightly' serious. This is perhaps reflected in the fact that age was the last of the nine characteristics to be protected (in 2006) and of course in the continued prevalence and acceptance by society of jokes about age, even on mainstream greetings cards.

Moreover, as part of the same study, the EHRC published a 'prejudice barometer' which suggested that 26% of adults in Britain have experienced some sort of age discrimination. This is the highest figure amongst all protected characteristics but is not reflected in the proportion of the number of claims brought in employment tribunals.

Whilst age discrimination is typically thought of as prejudicing older people, it can apply to those of any age. Stereotypes such as declining mental acuity, being 'out of touch' and a reduction in physical capability may be applied to older people whereas younger people may be unreasonably considered to be naïve, inexperienced and immature.

Age is also unusual in that it is the only protected characteristic for which there is a defence to direct discrimination of justification. This is usually only available in indirect discrimination cases. Although this in theory makes direct age discrimination cases easier to defend, statistical evidence submitted to a parliamentary subcommittee by Prof Alysia Blackham in November 2023 showed that in practice such a defence was only used in 7 out of 1208 age discrimination cases and only succeeded in one of those cases. This can be found at https://committees.parliament.uk/writtenevidence/126028/html/#_ftn42

In her study of tribunal decisions up until 2019 (*Enforcing rights in employment tribunals: insights from age discrimination claims in a new 'dataset'* – Legal Studies Vol 41), Prof Blackham also found that the median age of claimants was 57. This demonstrates the unsurprising fact that the majority of claims for age discrimination come from older people. However, it must not be forgotten that the law applies to all age groups – in November 2024, a survey commissioned by UK Youth and KFC of 9000 people aged 16-25 years found that over 90% had encountered negative treatment at work because of their age. Where we can, we have provided examples of discrimination against a variety of ages.

Scope of this book

This book is designed to cover all aspects of the various possible claims under Part 5 EqA – i.e. discrimination relating to work. We have focussed on employment relationships (in the Equality Act sense), which are the most prevalent type of claims under Part 5. It is not intended to provide guidance on discrimination in relation to education nor in relation to services and public functions. This said, the principles explained may provide a useful basis with which to understand the remainder of the EqA.

In chapters 2-4, we deal with direct and indirect age discrimination and how those claims can be justified. We go on to discuss harassment and victimisation in chapters 5 and 6. Chapter 7 discusses issues surrounding retirement such as a mandatory retirement age and how to discuss retirement plans with employees. We then go into more detail on the burden of proof in discrimination claims in chapter 8. Chapter 9 deals with the various remedies that are available in discrimination claims, including guidance on the various ways awards can be reduced. Chapter 10 – How to bring an age discrimination claim, provides details on who can claim and practical guidance on how claims proceed, from pleadings to hearings to appeals. Appendices 1 and 2 give examples of pleadings – particulars of claim and grounds of resistance in hypothetical age discrimination cases. Appendix 3 is a template list of issues, a document whose importance is often underestimated.

As noted above, we have tried to provide as many authentic case examples as possible in order to give readers a feel for how age discrimination claims work in reality. Readers are reminded however that tribunal judgments at first instance are not binding on other employment tribunals and that the same facts could lead to different outcomes with different tribunal judges.

How wide does protection from age discrimination extend?

Part 5 EqA explains both who is protected and who is liable for discrimination under that Part. Employees are of course the main subject of protection from discrimination. The definition of an employee is wider under the Equality Act than under other legislation such as the Employment Rights Act 1996 (which governs unfair dismissal amongst many other matters). Under section 83 EqA, the principal definition of employment is '*employment under a contract of employment, a contract of apprenticeship or a contract personally to do work*'. This covers a broad range of people including those described as 'workers' and contractors hired personally to do work. Please see Chapter 10 – How to bring an age discrimination claim, for more detail on who is protected and who is liable.

Protection from discrimination extends from the application process for jobs, all the way through employment to post-termination discrimination such as failing to respond to an appeal against dismissal or failing to give a reference due to the claimant's age.

Intersectionality

UK employment law focusses on discrimination related to or because of nine separate protected characteristics. Often however individuals may consider themselves to have been treated less favourably because they belong to a group with more than one protected characteristic. Such groups may include older women, young black men and older disabled people. Young black men, for example, may be subject to stereotypes and a combination of stigma that means they are treated worse than older black men, young white men and young white women. Although there is no prohibition (yet) in the EqA against this sort of combined discrimination, as explained in Chapter 2 Direct Age Discrimination, our view is that with selection of the right comparator, current discrimination law is highly likely to be sufficient to succeed on such claims, simply by claiming on the basis of three separate protected characteristics, further or in the alternative.

The idea of combined discrimination should be distinguished from circumstances in which claimants allege they have been subject to different types of discrimination on multiple protected characteristics. The former can be said to involve discrimination because of stigmatisation of specific groups with certain complex characteristics. The latter may often involve piecemeal allegations that an individual has been treated less favourably in a number of different instances for a number of different reasons that are not said to be connected. Victimisation and/or whistleblowing may also be added into the mix.

In our experience, tribunals will often raise an eyebrow at pleadings which allege that a claimant was subject to multiple acts of discrimination for different reasons or alternatively that one specific act was discrimination due to multiple protected characteristics. For example, an employee who alleges he was not promoted because the decision maker did not like middle-aged people, Hindus or disabled people and because he had raised a protected act. Claimants are unlikely to succeed on all four of those claims. As more reasons are added, it becomes more difficult to prove what the effective cause for the treatment was. In this way, a potentially strong claim could be undermined by a focus on three weaker claims. In other words, the claimant ends up falling between two (or more) stools. We therefore advise that claimants carefully consider which are their best arguments and put those forward.

One final category of intersectional case is where it is not clear upon which protected characteristic a claimant should rely because they overlap so much in that particular case. Less favourable treatment due to menopause may be said to be due to age, sex or disability (see Chapter 2 Direct Age Discrimination). Women over the age of 50 represented the fastest-growing group in the workforce, according to the '*Menopause and the workplace*' report published by the Women and Equalities Committee on 28th July 2022; yet the report also found that employers' lack of support for menopausal symptoms was pushing highly skilled and experienced older women out of the workforce. The protection of older women from prejudicial treatment and seeking to level the playing field to ensure they can make a valuable contribution to work in this country is likely to continue to remain an important issue, particularly given the recent media attention given to the menopause, thanks to celebrities like Davina McCall.

Prof Blackham's study (see above) found that when claims for age discrimination were pleaded with claims founded on other protected characteristics, the most common linked claims were for disability, sex and race. She noted in her evidence to parliament that age '*touches everything*' and exacerbates other forms of disadvantage, meaning that discrimination because of race or sex may be made worse by additional discriminatory attitudes about the age of the victim. These complexities are not necessarily reflected in statute but we feel that the guidance in this book shows that tribunals have the discretion and experience to make compensation reflect a wide range of factors.

Where is age discrimination heading?

The population of the UK is ageing due to increased life expectancy, falling birth rates, migration patterns and the legacy of a post-war baby boom. This demographic shift is reshaping our labour market. As the workforce in the UK grows older, both opportunities and challenges can be presented. Older individuals today are living longer, healthier lives, often with a desire—and in many cases, a need—to remain economically active well into what was once considered retirement age. As a result, the workforce is becoming increasingly age-diverse, spanning multiple generations, from school leavers to septuagenarians. However, with this growing age diversity comes a pressing need to confront the biases, stereotypes, stigma and systemic barriers that still persist in the world of work. Age discrimination—whether overt or subtle—remains a pervasive yet underacknowledged issue. While society has made progress in addressing inequalities around gender, race, and disability, ageism has historically too often been overlooked, treated as less urgent, or even accepted as an inevitable part of the employment experience.

More recently, age discrimination in the UK has garnered increased attention, highlighting both persistent challenges and emerging efforts to address them. The Women and Equalities Committee has called for stronger legal protections against age discrimination, including the appointment of a Commissioner for Older People's Rights in England, mirroring the model in Wales. According to the Financial Times ("*Age discrimination payouts are getting bigger*", published 20th February 2025), there was a surge in tribunal compensation awards to age discrimination claimants in 2022-2023, when the average pay-out reached £103,000 (the equivalent the previous year was £14,000). Although the 2022-2023 figure was based on only 12 cases, including some very senior executives, this underscores the financial and reputational risks employers face when neglecting age-related issues.

Justifying discrimination involves arguing that the act was done in order to achieve a legitimate aim. For mandatory retirement cases, the most oft cited and accepted aims are 'intergenerational fairness' and 'dignity' (see ***Seldon***). The former involves considerations of providing job opportunities for younger people and the latter refers to the notion that older employees should not be subject to what might be humiliating capability processes at the end of the career. It should be noted however that these aims ought to reflect the values of society and may therefore change over time. For example, one could argue that it is patronising and paternalistic to avoid capability processes for a particular age group and that it reflects assumptions that that group is less thick-skinned. Equally, with changes to life-expectancy and increased financial pressures for pensioners, it may not always be legitimate to expect older people to 'make way' for the younger generation.

However the law develops, what seems certain is that the importance and awareness of age discrimination is only going to increase.

<u>Sources</u>

The authors recommend to those encountering the law of age discrimination for the first time, and/or those making or facing age discrimination claims in the employment tribunal, to consult the excellent practical guidance available from ACAS and the Equality and Human Rights Commission, in particular:

https://www.acas.org.uk/age-discrimination

https://www.equalityhumanrights.com/equality/equality-act-2010/your-rights-under-equality-act-2010/age-discrimination

CHAPTER TWO

DIRECT AGE DISCRIMINATION

- *Identify the treatment or conduct complained of;*
- *Was (an) actual person or persons of a younger or older age treated more favourably?*
- *Would a hypothetical comparator who was older or younger be treated more favourably?*
- *If so, was this treatment because of age?*
- *Can the treatment be objectively justified –*
    - *Was the treatment a way of achieving a legitimate aim?*
    - *Was the treatment a proportionate way to achieve that aim, bearing in mind its discriminatory effect?*

Direct age discrimination, as outlined in Section 13 of the Equality Act 2010 ("EqA"), aims to safeguard individuals from less favourable treatment on the basis of their age. This provision prohibits any form of direct discrimination against individuals due to their age. Direct age discrimination occurs when an individual is treated less favourably because of their age, compared to how others in similar circumstances are or would be treated. This chapter examines the scope of direct age discrimination under Section 13 EqA.

The definition of direct age discrimination

Section 13 EqA (relevantly to age discrimination) provides:

> *Direct discrimination*
>
> *(1) A person (A) discriminates against another (B) if, because of a protected characteristic, A treats B less favourably than A treats or would treat others.*
>
> *(2) If the protected characteristic is age, A does not discriminate against B if A can show A's treatment of B to be a proportionate means of achieving a legitimate aim.*

Age is a protected characteristic under s.4 EqA.

Although the definition of direct discrimination under s.13(1) EqA usually involves split consideration of (a) less favourable treatment; and then (b) the reason for the treatment, tribunals sometimes find it impossible to deal with the questions separately. Lord Nicholls in ***Shamoon v Chief Constable of the Royal Ulster Constabulary*** [2003] ICR 337, HL commented that in some cases the *"less favourable treatment issue cannot be resolved without, at the same time, deciding the reason why issue. The two issues are intertwined"*. In that case a female police chief inspector had been relieved of her counselling responsibilities, whereas two male chief inspectors had not. She complained that, although there had been complaints against her, and not her comparators, the reason she had been less favourably treated was her sex. The question of whether the factual differences between the claimant and comparators were material to the decision to treat them in a certain way, involved considering both the reason for the treatment and whether an appropriate comparator would be treated more favourably.

Less favourable treatment

How unfavourable does the treatment have to be?

In order to establish less favourable treatment, the claimant has to have been subjected to something adverse to them, but the bar is set very low. According to the Statutory Code of Practice on Employment from the Equality and Human Rights Commission ("EHRC Code"), (see para.3.5) the claimant does not have to experience actual disadvantage (economic or otherwise) for the treatment to be less favourable. It is enough that the worker can *reasonably* say that they would have preferred not to be treated differently from the way the employer treated – or would have treated – another person. The inclusion of the word "reasonably" here, means that the test is objective. A claimant's belief that she has been less favourably treated is insufficient on its own to satisfy the objective test of whether, as a matter of fact, there has been less favourable treatment – see ***Burrett v West Birmingham Health Authority*** [1994] IRLR 7, EAT; though a claimant's perception is likely to be persuasive when the tribunal is determining whether or not the treatment amounted to some kind of detriment.

Theoretically, a glare from a colleague, if found to have been something which (a) a younger colleague would not have been subjected to, and (b) was done because of the older age of the person being glared at, could be actionable as direct age discrimination. Of course, such treatment would be difficult to prove, both in terms of the act itself and the causation of the act, and it is unlikely that any claimant would bother to take action over a single dirty look, given that the injury to feelings would be very low and no recoverable financial loss would flow from it.

"Banter" – a word which strikes fear into the hearts of respondent employment lawyers everywhere – can cause particular problems, usually in the context of harassment, dealt with in Chapter 5, but also in claims of direct age discrimination. Many workers enjoy joviality in the office, and sharing jokes to make their colleagues laugh can make the working day more tolerable. Age-related jokes can easily tip into the realm of less favourable treatment because of age, and therefore, at work, s.13 EqA can be engaged, regardless of the intention of the comedian. The tribunal must be satisfied, however, that the claimant did take offence in some way, and that it was reasonable for the joke to have that effect. In ***Dove v Brown and Newirth Ltd,*** ET Case No. 3301905/15, the new Head of Sales repeatedly called the claimant, who was the oldest member of the team, "*Gramps*". The respondent argued that it was an affectionate term of address, and not intended to cause harm, and therefore could not have reached the threshold of a detriment under s.13 (or under s.26 as a harassment claim, alternatively). The tribunal found that if the term had been used once or twice, it may not have been upheld, but using it more often led to a real detriment – saying the comment was "banter" was no defence.

It is important that there is something adverse to the claimant in the conduct complained of, even if is only making the claimant feel temporarily uncomfortable. In ***Keane v Investigo and ors*** EAT 0389/09, a person, aged 50, applied for various "newly qualified accountant" roles, but conceded she was not genuinely interested in undertaking the roles. She nevertheless argued that she had been subjected to age discrimination. Mr Justice Underhill, the President of the EAT, as he then was, found that direct discrimination required some kind of less favourable treatment, and it was not possible to see how an applicant who was not considered for a job in which she was not in any event interested could in any ordinary sense of the word be said to have suffered a detriment, or to have been comparatively unfavourably treated. The claimant in ***Keane*** was the subject of a costs order (see also ***Berry v Recruitment Revolution and ors*** EAT 0190/10, *per* Underhill P again).

A claimant with a genuine interest in a role, which has been advertised in a discriminatory way, such as to dissuade them from applying, can claim discrimination, as the effect of the advert would be detrimental to a genuine potential applicant.

As the EHRC Code sets out, (para.3.4) it is not possible for the employer to balance or eliminate less favourable treatment by offsetting it against more favourable treatment, for example, giving extra pay to make up for a loss of job status.

Unfavourable or less favourable treatment?

Unfavourable treatment is not enough to establish direct discrimination. If an employer treats people badly in general, that is a good defence to a direct discrimination claim (known by employment lawyers as "the bastard defence"). The use of the words "less favourable" requires a comparison to be undertaken. In the most straightforward case, there might be two employees, who are similarly trained, experienced and qualified, and who both commit the same misconduct. One is considerably older than the other and this employee is dismissed, whilst the other employee is simply given a written warning. This is an example of less favourable treatment than an actual comparator. Of course, less favourable treatment, because it is comparative, could also encompass a decision *not* to treat a person *more* favourably, like promoting one person instead of another.

Less favourable treatment will not be demonstrated by merely showing that a younger or older comparator was differently treated to the claimant – see ***Madarassy v Nomura International plc*** [2007] ICR 867, CA. In order to establish less favourable treatment, the comparator must be in similar circumstances to the claimant in all material respects, except age.

If there is no example of an actual comparator, meaning a person who was in fact more favourably treated than a claimant, the claimant can ask the tribunal to consider how the respondent would have treated a hypothetical person in materially the same circumstances of a different age. Even if there is an actual comparator, a hypothetical comparator could be used further to persuade the tribunal that the employer would treat people of a different age to the claimant more favourably.

Comparators (s.23 EqA)

Section 23 EqA relevantly states:

Comparison by reference to circumstances

(1) *On a comparison of cases for the purposes of section 13, 14, 19 or 19A there must be no material difference between the circumstances relating to each case.*

The EqA makes clear that a comparator need not be in identical circumstances to the claimant. What matters is that the circumstances which are relevant to the treatment of the worker are the same or nearly the same for the worker and the comparator – see paragraph 3.23 EHRC Code. Section 24 EqA makes clear it is irrelevant if the potential discriminator shares the protected characteristic with the claimant. It is sensible not to discount the possibility of less favourable treatment against people of the same age as the discriminator.

Different age

Of course, it is necessary in an age discrimination complaint, that the comparator is of a different age to the claimant. Generally, the more marked the difference in age between the claimant and the comparator, the more likely it is that discrimination will be established. It is theoretically possible for a comparator to be only a year different in age, but why would an employer treat a 37-year-old differently to a 38-year-old? The claimant might need to think very carefully about the age of the comparator. Is it a comparison with a comparator of a certain age range? E.g. a comparator could be above 40 years old, if there is alleged less favourable treatment of those in their 20s and 30s. Is it a comparator of a particular age? E.g. 18 year-old employees are given a Birthday Bonus, but employees of any other age are not. See Chapter 8 Proving age discrimination, for more detail on choosing a comparator.

The EAT have endorsed strike out, where the difference in age between the claimant and the comparator was only nine months, on the basis that prospects of success of demonstrating facts from which discrimination could be inferred were "fanciful" – ***ABN AMRO Management Services Ltd and anor v Hogben*** EAT 0266/09.

More recently, the EAT in ***Citibank NA and ors v Kirk*** [2022] EAT 103 considered a case where there was unchallenged evidence that the person deciding whom to appoint into a reorganised role perceived the claimant and his comparator to be the same age, despite the fact the claimant was four years older. The EAT found that the tribunal appeared not to have given due consideration to the Respondents' evidence in this regard, and to their explanation that age could not be the reason for the alleged discriminatory treatment. At paragraph 62 of the judgment of the Honourable Mr Justice Choudhury, he explained:

> *"Age discrimination can, therefore, arise where there is only a small difference in age between the person treated less favourably and his comparator. This is most likely to arise where the employer applies a particular age as a cut-off for some benefit or the imposition of some detriment. The person reaching the cut-off age may be subject to less favourable treatment whereas a person who is only a few weeks or months short of the cut-off age may not. However, in the absence of a cut-off age… a relatively small difference in age may render it less likely that the discriminatory treatment is because of age. Even then, the particular ages of those concerned might be relevant: a difference in age of two years between an 18- and 20-year-old might, for example, be considered much more significant than the same difference in age in those over the age of 40. A small difference in age between protagonists in their 50s might, without more, render it implausible that age is the reason for any difference in treatment. That is not to say that age could not be the reason in such cases, but a claim that it is would be subject to careful scrutiny".*

"No material difference" in circumstances

The situations of the comparator and the claimant do not have to be precisely the same. The Supreme Court has made it clear that whether the situations are sufficiently comparable is a question of fact and degree – ***Hewage v Grampian Health Board*** [2012] ICR 1054, SC. In ***Shamoon v Chief Constable of the Royal Ulster Constabulary*** [2003] ICR 337, the House of Lords found that the claimant's circumstances were comparable in many respects to her comparators – of the same rank, in the same branch and with similar responsibilities – but they were under the control of a different superintendent and they had not had any complaints levelled at them, whereas the claimant had. These individuals were therefore not appropriate comparators, because their circumstances were materially different.

In ***Kalu v Brighton and Sussex University Hospitals NHS Trust and ors*** EAT 0609/12 Mr Justice Langstaff, then President of the EAT stated (paragraphs 23 – 24)

> *"Circumstances are deliberately left undefined except by the word "relevant". This provides a very wide scope for the identification by a Tribunal of that which is relevant. Much depends on context.... The concept of "relevant circumstances" requires identification of that to which the circumstances in question are relevant: there must be a sufficient link in logic between the two if the Tribunal's conclusion of fact is to stand... The purpose of making the comparison thus needs to be understood before a comparator may properly be identified. It may often be convenient to address selection of the relevant circumstances by asking what proposition the comparison is intended to address. Where, for instance, it is that one of two candidates was favoured by discrimination over another for a job, the circumstances will be those which relate to suitability for employment in it."*

The examples given by Mr Justice Langstaff, in ***Kalu***, included a case concerning job applicants required to have intellectual skills, meaning the academic results of the claimant and the comparator would be relevant, but not their physical skills (ability to lift or to carry). The claimant in ***Kalu*** complained that the Trust treated the consultants at one hospital more favourably, because they were all white, than it treated the consultants at another hospital because they were mostly black. He therefore compared himself to the white consultants at the other hospital. The tribunal found that the comparators were not in materially the same circumstances because they were at different hospitals. The EAT found that was the incorrect approach to the comparator (although they found that the tribunal's finding that the reason for the treatment had nothing to do with race meant the claimant could not succeed on this claim anyway). The context of the question was whether a consultant at one hospital had been discriminated against on the grounds of race because of a policy adversely affecting those who were employed there. The location of the consultants was not a relevant material circumstance, so a difference in location between the comparator and the claimant did not render the comparator incorrect.

In the context of direct age discrimination, if there were two campuses of a university, for example, one (Campus A) at which younger lecturers were based, in comparison with another (Campus B) at which the lecturers were all over 40 years old, and a claimant, who was a 50-year-old lecturer and based at Campus B, complained that the facilities for lecturers at Campus A were better due to a university policy which prioritised the facilities at Campus A over those at Campus B, because of their younger age, ***Kalu*** makes clear that the base of the lecturers is probably not a material circumstance, for the purpose of identifying a suitable comparator. The comparison is (absent any other different material circumstances) between the claimant and the lecturers at Campus A, to determine whether there is any less favourable treatment. ***Kalu*** was appealed to the Court of Appeal but on different points, so Mr Justice Langstaff's comments still stand.

If two different people decided the treatment of the claimant and a comparator, that does not necessarily, on its own, amount to a material difference in their circumstances (see ***Olalekan v Serco Ltd*** [2019] IRLR 314, per Mr Justice Choudhury). Where the employer would be liable for the actions of both decision-makers, if a comparator was more favourably treated by Manager A than the claimant was by Manager B, where both the claimant and the comparator were in materially similar circumstances but significantly different ages, that could still amount to less favourable treatment by the employer. The focus would then be on the mental processes of the decision-maker who dealt with the claimant – was the reason for the treatment age? That is not to say that different decision-makers can never be a material difference between comparators, because it can be, particularly where each decision-maker is applying a different policy.

Actual, evidential or hypothetical comparators

Sometimes identifying an actual comparator is simple. Litigation could be contemplated because there is a person of a different age who is more favourably treated than the claimant, and there appears to be no explanation for that treatment, other than the difference in age. For example, a 20-year-old who doesn't receive a performance-based discretionary bonus, might seek to compare her treatment to her three colleagues all over the age of 50, who did receive bonuses, despite the fact that they all received identical performance feedback and had the same experience and training in their indistinguishable roles.

It is relatively rare, however, to find an individual who is in materially the same circumstances as someone else. Lord Hoffman considered that it is "*probably uncommon*" (in ***Watt (formerly Carter) and ors v Ahsan*** [2008] ICR 82, HL – a race discrimination case). What if there is no-one in a comparable position to the claimant?

It is not necessary for the comparator to be an actual person, a hypothetical comparator can be constructed instead. A claimant could rely, and is usually well-advised to rely, upon a hypothetical comparator, further or in the alternative to a named actual comparator, because an actual comparator sometimes turns out to have materially different circumstances to the claimant, which were not previously known to the claimant.

The EAT have found that the right approach to identifying the relevant circumstances of a comparator is to focus on the substance of the grievance in order to throw light on the material circumstances in a particular case. A female prison officer in ***Home Office v Saunders*** [2006] ICR 318, EAT, complained that male colleagues were not required to search female prisoners, whereas female officers were required to search male inmates. Had the comparison been between prison officers who were required to search male prisoners, there would have been no difference in treatment. Instead, the tribunal correctly compared the claimant to a hypothetical male colleague in circumstances where a prisoner of a different sex needed to be searched.

In the context of age discrimination, in ***Lockwood v Department of Work and Pensions and anor*** [2014] ICR 1257, the Court of Appeal cautioned tribunals against identifying material differences in circumstances which were nothing more than features of being a particular age. In that case, the claimant complained of direct age discrimination because, at the age of 26 years, she was paid a lower severance payment than a hypothetical 35 year-old who had also been made redundant after the same number of years' service, by virtue of the Civil Service Compensation Scheme. The tribunal considered that there would be a material difference in the circumstances of the claimant and her hypothetical comparator because those in their 20s had fewer financial and family obligations, and could react more easily and rapidly to the loss of their jobs. The Court of Appeal held that was the wrong approach on determining the comparator (although the finding of justification was upheld). The difference in circumstances was not relevant to the comparison because they were all factors consequent upon the claimant's age. The comparison had to be "*relevant, valid and essential*" for the purpose of determining whether the claimant had suffered less favourable treatment on the ground of age.

In ***Donkor v Royal Bank of Scotland*** [2016] IRLR 268, EAT, the claimant was denied the chance to apply for voluntary redundancy because, being 50, he would be entitled to early retirement benefits under the employer's pension scheme, whereas his younger colleagues were able to apply for voluntary redundancy. The EAT found that an entitlement to early retirement benefits was not a material difference in circumstances for the purpose of identifying comparators, because it was intrinsically linked to age.

Shamoon makes it clear that a comparator who does not satisfy the requirement that there be no material difference between his position and that of the claimant such that he cannot be a statutory comparator, can nonetheless be of some evidential value. However, that evidential value will be variable and will inevitably be weakened by material differences between the circumstances relating to them and the circumstances of the claimant.

If an actual comparator relied upon has very different circumstances, evidence of that nature is likely to assist a respondent in showing that those differences (and not age) were the reason for the more favourable treatment; whereas a comparator who cannot be considered in materially similar circumstances but whose differences are found not to have been operating on the mind of the employer, will assist the claimant to demonstrate that a hypothetical comparator would have been more favourably treated. This is known as an evidential comparator.

Recently, in ***Martin v Governors of St Francis Xavier 6th Form College*** [2024] IRLR 472 the EAT upheld the tribunal's view of comparators and Cavanagh J characterised comparators into three different categories:

(1) actual (or statutory) comparators – these are subject to the overall requirement in the EqA 2010 s23 that there must be no material differences with the position of the claimant;

(2) evidential comparators – these are where s23 is not satisfied, but there are still relevant similarities;

(3) hypothetical comparators – the question here is how they would have been treated and again s23 applies.

For example, even if everyone who works with a claimant has different circumstances, and are not therefore appropriate comparators, if they are all considerably older and have been treated more favourably than a claimant, a tribunal would be more likely to find that a hypothetical comparator in materially the same circumstances as the claimant, but older, would also have been more favourably treated. In essence, the tribunal would be finding that the different circumstances of the claimant's colleagues were not wholly causative of the more favourable treatment.

The EHRC Code (para. 3.26) states that constructing a hypothetical comparator may involve considering elements of the treatment of several people whose circumstances are similar to those of the claimant, but not the same. Looking at these elements together, an employment tribunal may conclude that the claimant was less favourably treated than a hypothetical comparator would have been treated. The EHRC also summarises the comparison by stating (at para.3.28):

> *"Another way of looking at this is to ask, 'But for the relevant protected characteristic, would the claimant have been treated in that way?'"*

The reason for the treatment

Less favourable treatment than a comparator is not sufficient to establish direct discrimination. It might be that a younger person has not been promoted despite being comparably qualified and in similar circumstances to an older person who was promoted, but if the tribunal find that the reason for the failure to promote had nothing to do with the age of the claimant, he will not succeed under s.13. For example, even where all the material circumstances are exactly the same between the two applicants for promotion, and the older one has been preferred, if the employer reveals that the decision between the two candidates was made on the flip of a coin, that would not be actionable as discrimination.

<u>The reason not being age itself</u>

If the reason for the treatment is not age itself but something inextricably linked to age, that is still likely to be "*because of age*" under s.13. For example, a worker being paid a lower bonus because they have less life experience than an older colleague, despite the fact that the younger person is better suited to the role and has more relevant experience and training, and has achieved better performance results, is likely to succeed in showing the treatment was because of age. Another example of something inextricably linked to age is probably menopause, so less favourable treatment because the person is menopausal is likely to be direct age discrimination. See ***Essop v Home Office (UK Border Agency) and Naeem v Secretary of State for Justice*** [2017] UKSC 27, in the context of indirect discrimination on the grounds of race, age or religion, and in the ECJ, ***MH Müller Handels GmbH v MJ***: C-341/19, [2021] IRLR 832; and "Menopause" below.

Age being only one of many reasons

Age need only be part of the reason for the treatment, not necessarily the only or main reason. It must be an operative cause, which means age made more than a trivial contribution to the cause of the treatment. The House of Lords in the race discrimination and victimisation case of ***Nagarajan v London Regional Transport*** [1999] IRLR 572, HL, also made clear that conscious motivation was not required for direct discrimination. Lord Nicholls opined (at paragraph 19):

> *"Decisions are frequently reached for more than one reason. Discrimination may be on racial grounds even though it is not the sole ground for the decision. A variety of phrases, with different shades of meaning, have been used to explain how the legislation applies in such cases: discrimination requires that racial grounds were a cause, the activating cause, a substantial and effective cause, a substantial reason, an important factor. No one phrase is obviously preferable to all others, although in the application of this legislation legalistic phrases, as well as subtle distinctions, are better avoided so far as possible. If racial grounds or protected acts had a significant influence on the outcome, discrimination is made out. Read in context, that was the industrial tribunal's finding in the present case. The tribunal found that the interviewers were 'consciously or subconsciously influenced by the fact that the applicant had previously brought tribunal proceedings against the respondent."*

Inherently discriminatory / reason why

Sometimes the cause of the treatment will be obvious. If an advertisement expressly states an age bracket for applicants, like, "*Only applicants between 18 and 25 years' old need apply*", a 30-year-old applicant who was not interviewed will probably easily persuade a tribunal that the reason he was not offered an interview, in part, was his older age. In this example, the reason for the treatment is inherent in the act itself, and the tribunal need not examine the mental processes of the decision-maker.

The "but for" test is not a helpful way of understanding the test for causation under s.13. What this means is that, even if it can be said that *but for* a claimant's particular age, she would not have been treated in the less favourable way, this does not mean the treatment was necessarily because of her age – see ***Gould v St John's Downshire Hill*** [2020] IRLR 863. As Underhill P (as he then was) stated in ***Amnesty International v Ahmed*** [2009] ICR 1450 at paragraph 37,

> "*The fact that a claimant's* [age]... *is a part of the circumstances in which the treatment complained of occurred, or of the sequence of events leading up to it, does not necessarily mean that it formed part of the ground, or reason, for that treatment*" (our substitution of protected characteristic).

In many, if not most, cases, the link between the treatment and age is not overt or obvious and it becomes necessary to analyse the reasons operating on the mind of the decision-maker. Sometimes age is an operative cause of treatment without the decision-maker being aware that it is. Unconscious bias is as unlawful as conscious bias. It is a matter of fact for the tribunal to decide whether age was an operative cause of the treatment, consciously or unconsciously.

Motive is irrelevant

It matters not if the decision-maker makes a well-intentioned decision which results in less favourable treatment because of age; such a decision, as long as it is in some way objectively adverse to a claimant, is still likely to be discriminatory and unlawful. In ***Amnesty International v Ahmed*** [2009] IRLR 884 the organisation was seeking to protect its impartiality, and thus its effectiveness, and avoid unacceptable security risks involved in appointing the claimant, but was still found to have discriminated against her because of her race.

Stereotypes

Direct age discrimination is also made out where a worker is less favourably treated because of a stereotype related to their age, even if that stereotype is accurate (***R (on the application of the European Roma Rights Centre) v Immigration Officer at Prague Airport*** [2004] UKHL 55). Not inviting an older colleague to a work party, on the assumption that they would not like the loud music because they are older, is likely to be directly discriminatory.

In ***Imperial College Healthcare NHS Trust v Matar*** [2023] EAT 1, [2023] IRLR 264, both the claimant in his late 50s and a younger colleague were found to be underqualified for their roles. The younger employee was offered training and a lower-grade post in the meantime, whereas there were discussions about early retirement with the claimant because it was assumed he would not be interested in taking the more junior role temporarily. The EAT confirmed that the tribunal was justified in concluding that this age-related assumption was direct discrimination.

Focus on the mind of the decision-maker

Where a decision-maker has been influenced by the ageist actions of others, without knowing that those actions are ageist, that discriminatory cause cannot be attributed to the decision-maker herself. For example, if a manager, A, does not like a particular colleague, B, because B is considerably younger, so A fabricates grounds for disciplinary action against B, then a different manager, C, who decides to dismiss B on the basis of the fabricated grounds, without knowing they are fabricated or why, cannot be said to have discriminated against B by dismissing him. Only if C dismisses A, consciously or unconsciously, because of his age, is the dismissal discriminatory. In ***Reynolds v CLFIS (UK) Ltd*** [2015] ICR 1010, CA, Lord Justice Underhill stated:

> *'the individual employee who did the act complained of must himself have been motivated by the protected characteristic. I see no basis on which his act can be said to be discriminatory on the basis of someone else's motivation'.*

The position is different to liability for unfair dismissal or unlawful detriment due to whistleblowing (see ***Royal Mail Group Ltd v Jhuti*** [2019] UKSC 55). The EAT have decided that the ***Reynolds*** approach is the correct one in relation to actions under the EqA in ***Alcedo Orange Ltd v Ferridge-Gunn*** [2023] EAT 78.

Of course, a claimant could claim that they have been the victim of an age-discriminatory act, short of dismissal, where a colleague unfairly causes their dismissal because of age, as in the example given above, and their employer would (subject to the statutory defence) be vicariously liable for the actions of that colleague (under s.109 EqA). The compensation might also be the same, since it could probably be established that the loss of earnings did flow from the act of fabricating grounds for the dismissal. There might be limitation problems or difficulties identifying the discriminator, and it is a little incongruous that there might be different results on an unfair dismissal case, and a discriminatory dismissal claim where a discriminator has caused the dismissal without being the decision-maker.

Association with or perception of age

The reason for the treatment must be age, in order to constitute age discrimination, but it need not be the age of the claimant. If the reason for the claimant's treatment is the age of someone with whom the claimant is associated, or the perceived age of the claimant, s.13 is still engaged.

Direct age discrimination by association

The association with the person who has the protected characteristic does not have to be familial, or any particular association. Whether the claimant's association with someone with the protected characteristic was the cause of the treatment is simply a matter of fact for the tribunal to determine. The EAT in ***Thompson v London Central Bus Co*** [2016] IRLR 9 (a case under s.27 EqA on victimisation) found that membership of a trade union by both the claimant and the individuals performing the relevant protected act could be a sufficient basis for a successful victimisation claim, as long as the reason for the treatment was the protected act. This applies equally under s.13. HHJ Tayler in ***Bennett v Mitac Europe Ltd*** [2022] IRLR 25, EAT, (paragraph 38), stated:

> *"The use of terms such as "associative discrimination" and "discrimination by perception" are not the key to the analysis. The real question is whether the protected characteristic of the other person was an effective cause of the treatment of B."*

Oft-seen examples of associative age discrimination relate to carers or partners. For example, if a claimant has a partner who is considerably older than them, and the claimant is less favourably treated because of their partner's age, that is likely to constitute direct age discrimination. If a claimant is less favourably treated because they have young children, this is also likely to be caught by s.13.

It should be borne in mind that there is a specific exception to associative age discrimination, contained in paragraph 15, Sch 9 EqA. It is expressly not age discrimination by association where employers only provide or make arrangements for or facilitate *"the provision of, care for children of a particular age group"*. A "*child*" is any child under the age of 17 — para 15(4).

Direct age discrimination by perception

Where someone has been less favourably treated not because of their age but because of the age they are perceived to be by the perpetrator, s.13 is still engaged. In ***Chief Constable of Norfolk v Coffey*** [2019] IRLR 805, a police constable with some hearing loss, but who was not statutorily disabled, was refused a transfer because the Inspector perceived her to be disabled (by way of a progressive condition), and therefore someone who might be restricted in her duties in future. Despite the fact she was not disabled herself, the constable succeeded in showing that she had been subjected to less favourable treatment because of disability.

Similarly, in a sexual orientation harassment case, before the EqA was enacted, the Court of Appeal, in ***English v Thomas Sanderson Blinds Ltd*** [2008] EWCA Civ 1421, found that a man, who was known not to be gay, was nevertheless subjected to unwanted conduct on the ground of homosexual orientation.

To give an example in the context of age, a person who looks youthful and is therefore treated like the baby of a group of workers, to his detriment, even though he is the same age as his colleagues, could still claim direct age discrimination.

Combined discrimination

Although s.14 of the EqA sets out that it is unlawful for a person to be less favourably treated because of a combination of two relevant protected characteristics, that provision has never been in force, and there are no published plans to bring this into force. This means that, theoretically, if an employer only treats an employee badly because of a combination of two protected characteristics, and would not treat an employee badly who only had one of the characteristics, a claimant could not succeed in a discrimination claim. In reality, this section adds little to the current law.

Consider the example of an employer (X) who acts in accordance with the racist and ageist stereotype that young black men are more likely to be violent. X does not promote a young black man (Y) because of his young age and his race, but he would have promoted a white man of the same age and/or an older black man. X might argue that Y was not less favourably treated (because of race) than the hypothetical older person because they are of the same colour; and Y was not less favourably treated (because of age) than the hypothetical white man because they are the same age. Y would be well advised to present both direct race and direct age discrimination claims. Y should construct alternative hypothetical comparators of:

(1) a white man of a similar age (because age is a material circumstance) who would have been promoted, for his direct race discrimination claim; and/or

(2) a black man of an older age (because race is a material circumstance) who would have been promoted, for his direct age discrimination claim.

As long as either protected characteristic was an effective cause of the loss of promotion (given that neither protected characteristic would have to be the main or only cause), and his comparator would have been successful, his claims should succeed.

The case of ***Jolly v Royal Berkshire NHS Foundation Trust*** ET Case No. 3324869/2017, concerned an 86-year-old NHS secretary who was discriminated against and harassed because of her age and disability. Despite an excellent sickness absence record, managers made decisions about her future and ultimately dismissed her due to stereotypical assumptions about her frailty and supposed inability to retrain. The tribunal found that there was a "*symbiosis*" between Mrs Jolly's age and disability in the way she was treated – i.e. she suffered less favourable treatment in relation to stereotypes about frailty which were related to both her age and her disabilities. This meant she succeeded on both claims. It may not always be possible to separate out whether less favourable treatment is because of one protected characteristic or another but this will not necessarily be a bar to success, as long as both protected characteristics are effective causes.

Menopause

A commonly encountered example of a claim which would be caught by s.14, if ever it was brought into force, is a claim concerning the menopause.

As it usually affects only women who are also older, it could be said that treatment which is less favourable to people experiencing the menopause is directly discriminatory because of a combination of age and sex. Arguably menopause is so intrinsically linked to both age and sex, a direct discrimination claim is possible.

Again, the fact that section 14 EqA is not in force is unlikely to be a bar to liability in a menopause case because a comparator could be constructed to establish liability under s.13. A tribunal dealing with an employer treating menopausal women less favourably, is likely to be unsympathetic to an employer who seeks to defend this treatment on the basis that they would not have treated a younger woman in an unfavourable way, or a man of a similarly advanced age in an unfavourable way. Such a tribunal is likely to find (a) it is age discrimination, because a younger person in materially the same circumstances would have been treated more favourably; (b) it is sex discrimination, because a man in materially the same circumstances, including being the same age, would be treated more favourably; or (c) it is both age and sex discrimination because both age and sex were operative causes of the less favourable treatment. Neither protected characteristic has to be the main or principal cause of the treatment to be actionable (see ***Nagarajan*** above).

A complaint concerning a menopausal woman being placed at a disadvantage by a certain practice or practices in her workplace would be well-advised to consider a claim of indirect age (and/or sex) discrimination (see Chapter 3 Indirect age discrimination).

Interestingly, in relation to the menopause, many women could be said to have a statutory disability within the definition of s.6 EqA, if the symptoms of the menopause have a substantial (meaning more than trivial) and long-term (meaning likely to last or recur over at least a year) adverse effect on her ability to carry out normal day-to-day activities (see ***Rooney v Leicester City Council*** [2022] IRLR 17, EAT). If, in her particular circumstances, the menopause constituted a statutory disability, her employer would be under a duty to make reasonable adjustments (under ss.20-21 EqA), and not to treat her unfavourably, without objective justification, for any reason which arose in consequence of the menopause (under s.15 EqA). The protection for disabled people is wider than the protection afforded to other protected characteristics, so it would be advisable for menopausal women with such a claim to consider whether their claim could be framed as one of disability discrimination, in addition to or as an alternative to a sex / age discrimination claim.

The Women and Equalities Committee published their "*Menopause and the workplace*" report on 28 July 2022 and identified that women over the age of 50 represented the fastest-growing group in the workforce, and that employers' lack of support for menopausal symptoms was pushing highly skilled and experienced women out of work. The government rejected its proposal to amend the EqA to introduce a new protected characteristic of menopause, but working with older women in the workplace to ensure they are not less favourably treated is likely to continue to be a hot topic. There is some helpful specific guidance from ACAS and EHRC, which is outside the scope of this book.

https://www.acas.org.uk/menopause-at-work

https://www.equalityhumanrights.com/guidance/menopause-work place-guidance-employers

Justification

Direct age discrimination is the only form of direct discrimination which can be lawfully justified. Section 13 makes clear it is for the perpetrator of the less favourable treatment because of age to prove that their treatment was a proportionate means of achieving a legitimate aim. It is more difficult to justify direct discrimination, than indirect discrimination. The requisite legitimate aims are narrowly confined to ones of labour market and social policy, rather than the wider aims of an individual employer.

Determining proportionality is a balancing exercise. The business need must be balanced against the discriminatory effect of the treatment. Although the employer does not have to show that the claimant's treatment was the only way of achieving the aim, in general, if a less discriminatory measure would have achieved the aim, it is unlikely that the treatment will be found proportionate. Justification is dealt with in more detail in Chapter 4.

Other defences to direct age discrimination

Positive action

In addition to the defence of justification being available in direct discrimination cases, employers can seek to defend some action which is because of age if it constitutes "positive action". In summary, sections 158-159 EqA mean that the law, in some circumstances, permits what would otherwise be age discrimination, if the employer is aiming to help a worker or an applicant because of age. Positive action is supposed to be used to level the playing field (as opposed to giving an advantage to a certain age group) and can help organisations become more diverse and representative. Employers must be careful to operate within the parameters of the EqA because overstepping those parameters can easily trespass into unlawful discrimination.

Where an employer reasonably thinks that workers / applicants of a certain age suffer a disadvantage connected to their age, or have different needs because of their age, or are underrepresented in the organisation or in participating in a particular activity, an employer can help those workers to overcome the disadvantage, to meet their needs or to participate, as applicable. Lawful assistance can only go so far as is proportionate.

For example, if an employer finds that the majority of workers over the age of 50 years, were struggling to get to grips with a new social media focus of their roles, a training scheme on social media, aimed at older employees, could be introduced to assist them.

Specifically in relation to recruitment and promotion, if a certain age group is underrepresented within a company, an employer could identify a way to encourage people of the underrepresented age to apply for certain roles. For example, advertising vacancies in magazines with a readership of the under-represented age could encourage more of those people to apply. It is important that no detriment is caused to any other age group applying, but if vacancies are advertised in a variety of places, it is unlikely that this advertisement would be detrimental to any other age group, and the action would therefore be proportionate.

In rare circumstances, and only as a last resort to address under-representation of a certain age group, age can be used as a tie-breaker where two candidates for a particular role are of equal merit. This type of positive action is only permissible if it is a proportionate way of overcoming or minimising the relevant disadvantage / under-representation. This means that it will be direct age discrimination if an employer appoints a 55 year-old candidate, who is only the third best candidate, because he believes older people are underrepresented in the workplace. Despite the desire for diversity in the workplace, this is not a tie-breaker situation and so such a decision is unlawful.

At the time of writing, the authors are unaware of any reported cases which has dealt with the defence of positive action in an age discrimination case. This is probably because direct age discrimination can lawfully be justified and objective justification is usually easier for an employer to demonstrate than positive action.

Occupational requirement

Positive action is to be distinguished from positive age discrimination, that is, more favourable treatment because of age, to the detriment of another age group. Positive age discrimination is unlawful except where it amounts to an occupational requirement. There is a general exception under the EqA to the prohibition on direct discrimination if it can be shown that certain characteristics are necessary occupational requirements. For example, if a child actor is required for a role, a certain age bracket is likely to be necessary for the actor in question. Schedule 9 of the EqA is given effect by s.83(11).

Paragraph 1(1) of Schedule 9 EqA states that,

> *"A person (A) does not contravene a provision mentioned in sub-paragraph (2) by applying in relation to work a requirement to have a particular protected characteristic, if A shows that, having regard to the nature or context of the work:*
>
> *(a) it is an occupational requirement,*
>
> *(b) the application of the requirement is a proportionate means of achieving a legitimate aim, and*
>
> *(c) the person to whom A applies the requirement does not meet it (or A has reasonable grounds for not being satisfied that the person meets it)".*

The exception only applies where the occupational requirement ("OR") is for the protected characteristic itself. This is slightly different to the EU Equality Directives where the exception is wider – an OR could merely be related to the protected characteristic. In ***Wolf v Stadt Frankfurt am***

Main [2010] IRLR 244, the ECJ held that imposing an age limit on applications to join the Fire Service was defensible under Article 4(1) of the Framework Directive. It accepted that physical fitness was a characteristic related to age for the purposes of Article 4(1) and that the possession of "*especially high physical capacities*" was a genuine occupational requirement. It went on to find that the requirement was justified on the basis that frontline work in the Fire Service requires a high level of physical capacity, which inevitably declines with age (see also ***Sorondo v Academia Vasca de Policía y Emergencias*** [2017] ICR 302, ECJ, concerning the Basque Country police force). If the same factual cases were to be decided under our domestic law, the results would likely be different, because age itself was not the requirement, fitness was, which was related to age. It is easy to see how the wider exception sanction under the EU Directives could conceal a stereotypical view of age-related deterioration.

The Explanatory Notes to the EqA support the more stringent approach of the EqA to the exception, stating that an OR must be "*crucial to the post, and not merely one of several important factors*" (see para 787).

The purported OR also needs to be objectively justified. In relation to age discrimination, because it is the only form of direct discrimination which can be justified, it is unlikely that an employer would bother to rely upon the OR exception, which also needs to be a proportionate means of achieving a legitimate aim, in addition to establishing that it is a genuine OR, rather than simply seeking to justify direct discrimination.

There are other general defences and exceptions to age discrimination claims, like:

- National Minimum Wage / National Living Wage, having different rates for those aged below 25 years (see www.acas.org.uk/national-minimum-wage-entitlement);

- Redundancy pay, being partially based on the age of the employee;

- Pay and extra job benefits (especially life assurance or health insurance) linked to time with employer or State pension age (see The Employment Equality (Repeal of Retirement Age Provisions) Regulations 2011, SI 2011/1069, and Chapter 3 Indirect age discrimination). Additional pay and benefits linked to up to 5 years' service generally do not need to be objectively justified;

- Pensions – a complex area, where potential claimants may well be assisted by the Pensions Advisory Service or a regulated financial adviser (see also The Equality Act (Age Exceptions for Pension Schemes) Order 2010 SI 2010/2133);

- Restrictions on employing workers below the age of 18;

- By providing or making arrangements for or facilitating the provision of, care for children of a particular age group – EqA 2010 Sch 9 para 15(1);

- Safeguarding national security (under section 192 EqA); or

- Relating to the armed forces (see paragraph 4(3) of Schedule 9 of the EqA and s.83 EqA).

The detail of these is outside the scope of this book.

CHAPTER THREE

INDIRECT AGE DISCRIMINATION

- *Identify a provision, criterion or practice ('PCP') that is applied to a group of people which includes different age groups.*

- *Does the PCP particularly disadvantage the claimant's age group compared to others?*

- *Is the claimant themselves put at this disadvantage?*

- *If so, can the Respondent justify the PCP i.e. show that it was a proportionate means of achieving a legitimate aim?*

Introduction

The provisions relating to indirect age discrimination are set out in s19 Equality Act 2010 ('EqA'). The section aims to protect individuals from provisions, criteria or practices that have a greater negative impact on certain age groups than on others.

In ***Chief Constable of West Yorkshire Police and another v Homer*** [2012] UKSC 15/[2012] ICR 704, SC, one of the most important cases on indirect discrimination, the Supreme Court defined indirect discrimination as '*an attempt to level the playing field by subjecting to scrutiny requirements which look neutral on their face but in reality work to the comparative disadvantage of people with a particular protected characteristic.*' (para 17).

If the employer can justify those requirements by showing it had a legitimate aim and that the policy was a proportionate means of achieving that legitimate aim, then this will be a complete defence to the claim. This is known as justification and is dealt with in the following chapter.

This chapter looks at the key elements of proving and defending an indirect age discrimination claim, along with examples and practical tips.

Statutory framework – definition of indirect discrimination

S19 EqA 2010 provides as follows:

> ***Indirect discrimination***
>
> *(1) A person (A) discriminates against another (B) if A applies to B a provision, criterion or practice which is discriminatory in relation to a relevant protected characteristic of B's.*
>
> *(2) For the purposes of subsection (1), a provision, criterion or practice is discriminatory in relation to a relevant protected characteristic of B's if—*
>
> > *(a) A applies, or would apply, it to persons with whom B does not share the characteristic,*
> >
> > *(b) it puts, or would put, persons with whom B shares the characteristic at a particular disadvantage when compared with persons with whom B does not share it,*
> >
> > *(c) it puts, or would put, B at that disadvantage, and*
> >
> > *(d) A cannot show it to be a proportionate means of achieving a legitimate aim.*

What is a Provision, Criterion or Practice ('PCP')?

The notion of a PCP should be construed widely. It can include '*any formal or informal policies, rules, practices, arrangements, criteria, conditions, prerequisites, qualifications or provisions*' (EHRC Employment:

Code of Practice). It may even include an employer's expectation (***United First Partners Research v Carreras*** [2018] EWCA Civ 323, at 35).

Although a general or habitual approach by the employer is enough (***Williams v Governing Body of Alderman Davies Church in Wales Primary School*** [2020] IRLR 589), even a one-off decision may constitute a PCP – ***Starmer v British Airways Plc*** [2005] IRLR 862 EAT.

In the context of this book, the following examples of pleaded PCPs in indirect age discrimination cases may assist in explaining the broad nature of the concept:

- A requirement to take a particular test to be promoted. This was harder for older people to pass and so older people failed more. ***Essop and others v Home Office (UK Border Agency); Naeem v Secretary of State for Justice*** [2017] IRLR 558 SC.

- Requirements to move objects up to 25kg with assistance and be predominantly on one's feet in the mornings. This was argued to be harder for older people. ***Tucker v Gaiger Brothers*** ET 1404339/2023.

- Requirements of 'recent experience' of private practice and experience working at a Big Four accountancy firm. It was argued younger people were more likely to have that recent experience and so older people were disadvantaged. ***Johnson v Dunelm (Soft Furnishings) Ltd*** ET 6000079/2022.

- A policy that promoted employees are picked from a 'Talent Pool'. Statistics showed that older people were less likely to be in the Talent Pool. ***Ryan v South West Ambulance Services NHS Trust*** UKEAT/0213/19.

- A requirement still to be employed on a particular date in order to receive a bonus. This was said to affect people near retirement more than younger people. ***Mr A Fasano v (1) Reckitt Benckiser Group Plc (2) Reckitt Benckiser Health Ltd*** [2024] EAT 7.

- A policy of compulsory retirement for police officers who had reached 30 years of service. This could only apply to officers over 48. ***Chief Constable of West Midlands Police and others v Harrod and others*** [2017] ICR 869.

- A policy that redundancy payments increased according to length of service. This meant that younger employees would receive less than older employees when made redundant. ***MacCulloch v Imperial Chemical Industries plc*** [2008] ICR 1334.

- A policy that employees who were entitled to benefits under the company pension scheme were no longer entitled to contractual redundancy payments. This meant that those over 60 received no redundancy payments. ***Loxley v BAE Systems Land Systems (Munitions & Ordnance) Ltd*** [2008] ICR 1334.

It is clear that much of the reported case law involves discrimination against older people. The following are hypothetical examples which could involve discrimination of different age groups:

- A requirement that employees own a car. This may affect younger people who may be less likely to own a car.

- A policy that individuals must have ten years of work experience to be a mentor. This will likely disadvantage younger people who have not had enough years working to achieve that.

- A requirement to do mandatory weekend retreats. Those in their 30s and 40s with childcare responsibilities may not be able to comply as easily as those below 30 or above 50.

- A policy that core hours are fixed at 9-4pm. This may discriminate against those in their 30s and 40s who may be more likely to need to pick up children from school.

- Requirement to be a 'digital native'. This expression tends to mean someone who has grown up with computers and smartphones. That is likely to exclude anyone over about 40 and so is likely to disadvantage that group.

- Practice of networking during a work cross-fit club. A work cross-fit club may be more likely to be attended by those under 55. If there is a practice of a manager favouring those who attend for promotion or better work, then this may disadvantage older people.

<u>A PCP can be actual disadvantage or potential disadvantage</u>

Regarding the difference in 19(2)(c) between '*puts*' and '*would put*', the explanatory notes to the EqA describe two types of PCP. They can be described as (1) actual disadvantage and (2) potential disadvantage.

First, a policy that has been applied in the same way to everybody but has an effect which in fact has disadvantaged people of a certain age group. For example, a 23 year-old claimant works for a company that has a policy which states that it only allows those who have ten years of work experience to participate in a bonus scheme. This means that he, and other employees under 25, are not paid a bonus. This would constitute a PCP which likely disadvantages the 18-25 year-old category more than other ages. It is actual disadvantage.

Secondly, a policy which *would* put a particular age group at a disadvantage if applied. For example, a 23 year-old that is put off applying to the same company because it does not allow employees with fewer than ten years' experience to participate in the company bonus scheme. Members of the 18-25 year-old category may be deterred from applying because of the lack of bonus. This is potential disadvantage.

It is worth remembering that although potential disadvantage is valid as a PCP, it may be more difficult to evidence than actual disadvantage.

A PCP can sometimes be a one-off decision

Although it might seem that a PCP can only work if it can be shown to have been applied to a wide group of people, this is not necessarily the case.

In ***Starmer***, the claimant was a female pilot who asked to work 50% hours due to childcare issues. She was refused and was told she needed to work at least 75% due to business reasons (e.g inability to reorganise her work amongst colleagues). The general policy was that employees could in fact apply for 50% or 75% contracts and there was evidence that there were many colleagues who had been given 50% contracts. So Mrs Starmer could not argue that there was a PCP applied to all employees that they had to work at least 75%.

The EAT agreed that the decision in her case was a 'provision' and that it was a provision that did not apply to others. Nevertheless, it could be extrapolated to others. In other words, if the employer would have applied this to others in the same situation, then it can constitute a PCP.

The Court of Appeal came to a similar conclusion on how to deal with one-off decisions in ***Ishola v Transport for London*** [2020] IRLR 368, albeit on the facts of that case, it found that there was no PCP because it would not have been applied to others [paras 37-38]. The PCP in that case regarded not investigating Mr Ishola's grievance fairly.

The different treatment of the two cases shows that when formulating a PCP, it is important to think about whether the conduct in question is something that the employer has done or would do again in a similar situation. If it is not, indirect discrimination may not be the appropriate head of claim.

Establishing a PCP

It is important to think carefully about how to word the PCP – there may be multiple options available arising from the same conduct, some of which may be accepted as PCPs and some which will not be accepted and thus cause a claim to fail. A potential claimant will also need to consider how to define the age or age group that is being disadvantaged disproportionately compared to another age group.

For example, an employee that has been made redundant and suspects that age has something to do with it because she sees that a disproportionate number of similar aged colleagues doing her role have also been made redundant. A good PCP could simply be '*the application of the selection criteria for redundancy*'. A PCP of '*a policy of making older people redundant*' will fail because it is not a PCP that applies to different age groups (albeit it may succeed as a direct discrimination claim). It may also be difficult to evidence that it was a policy – the fact that older people were made redundant is the effect of the PCP, not the PCP itself.

<u>The pool for comparison</u>

The PCP will apply to a certain set of individuals, including the claimant. This set is known as the 'pool'. It is important to identify it correctly. The individuals in the pool and the claimant must be in materially the same circumstances, aside from their age (s23(1) EqA). Some of them will be disadvantaged by the PCP and some will not be. These parameters then allow for a fair assessment of whether the age group of the claimant is disadvantaged, compared to another age group which is not. In the seminal indirect discrimination case of ***Essop and others v Home Office (UK Border Agency); Naeem v Secretary of State for Justice*** [2017] IRLR 558 SC, Lady Hale confirmed these points and explained that the PCP effectively identifies the pool because the pool should encompass all the individuals to whom the PCP applies (paras 40-42). A pool could be anything from a few people to a whole organisation and will depend on the way the PCP is framed.

PCP must apply neutrally to more than one age group

As above, the PCP must apply to both the age group of the individual bringing the claim and the comparator age group. If the PCP only applies to one age group, then there can be no disadvantage to one group compared to another. In the ET case of ***Walker v London Borough of Lewisham*** ET Case No. 2301162/2020, the claimant attempted to claim indirect age discrimination because of a policy that prevented employees from continuing full-time in the same job once they had started to draw their pension. The major flaw in the PCP was that it only applied to those who were receiving their pension. This meant he could not show the PCP disadvantaged older people compared to younger people.

No need to demonstrate why the PCP disadvantages a particular age group

Unlike direct discrimination, there is no need to demonstrate a causal link between the PCP and age. As the Supreme Court in ***Essop*** found, it is '*not necessary to establish the reason for the particular disadvantage to which the group is put*' [para 33]. In the case of age, this means that it does not matter why a PCP disadvantages people of a certain age group, as long as it does. In the case of ***Ryan v South West Ambulance Services NHS Trust*** UKEAT/0213/19, the Respondent operated a 'Talent Pool' which identified future leaders of various grades, making them more likely to be promoted. Ms Ryan complained that this was a PCP which was indirectly discriminatory because there were only half the number of 55–70 year-olds in the pool as would be expected. It did not matter why that was the case or what created the link to age. It was enough that the statistics showed an underrepresentation. The reason behind this, as Lady Hale stated in ***Essop*** is that indirect discrimination aims to deal with '*hidden barriers which are not easy to anticipate or to spot*'. Proving a causal connection to age would be too onerous on claimants.

Intention is irrelevant

Indirect discrimination can often be entirely unintentional. In the *Ryan* case, there was no need for the claimant to establish that older people were not being put in the Talent Pool due to their age. It was enough simply that there was a lower proportion of people above 55.

Concessions

Respondents should give consideration to whether to concede a PCP and/or a particular disadvantage. Tactically it can sometimes be better to do this and focus on arguing justification rather than putting forward technical arguments on PCP and disadvantage. Many of the cases on indirect age discrimination do in fact revolve around issues of legitimate aim and proportionality, the employer having conceded the first stages of the legal test.

What is a particular disadvantage?

The notion of particular disadvantage comes directly from European law. Article 2 of Directive 2000/78/EC expressly refers to the phrase in the definition of indirect discrimination:

> *(b) indirect discrimination shall be taken to occur where an apparently neutral provision, criterion or practice would put persons having a particular religion or belief, a particular disability, a particular age, or a particular sexual orientation at a particular disadvantage compared with other persons unless [it can be justified]*

The case of ***Chez Razpredelenie Bulgaria Ad V. Komisia Za Zashtita Ot Diskriminatsia* Case C-83/14** [2015] IRLR 746 provided some useful guidance on this wording, albeit in the context of an indirect race discrimination case. It found that a particular disadvantage does *not* have to be serious, obvious or particularly significant [para 99]. Further, no particular degree of seriousness is necessary [para 103].

It is a wide concept. Indeed, the definition under the EqA allows for a less strict test than the previous law on discrimination did under various different acts. The EHRC code states that it includes denial of an opportunity or choice, deterrence, rejection or exclusion and compares it to the notion of 'detriment' [para 4.9] – see Chapter 2 on direct age discrimination.

<u>The disadvantage must be related to age</u>

Although, as mentioned above, there is no need to explain *why* a PCP creates a disadvantage for people of a certain age group, it is still necessary to demonstrate that the particular age group is disadvantaged.

In the case of ***Homer***, one of the seminal cases on indirect discrimination, and an age case itself, the claimant was a retired police officer working as a legal adviser for West Yorkshire Police. When he was appointed, a law degree was not an essential requirement for his post. Indeed, he had many years of experience in criminal law. Subsequently, the Respondent applied a new policy – that in order to achieve the highest grade of that role, a law degree was necessary. Mr Homer was in his early 60s. This meant there would not be time for him to complete a law degree before the force's mandatory retirement age of 65. He did not therefore have time to achieve the highest grade/promotion in the same way as someone in a similar position who was younger.

The Court of Appeal held that the reason for the disadvantage was impending retirement and not age *per se.* The Supreme Court (Lady Hale) disagreed, stating: '*a requirement which works to the comparative disadvantage of a person approaching compulsory retirement age is indirectly discriminatory on grounds of age*' (Para 17).

The Supreme Court decided that Mr Homer had satisfied the first three parts of the test – i.e. that there was (1) a PCP applied which (2) disadvantaged people of his age more than younger colleagues and (3) disadvantaged him personally. Lady Hale reasoned that the particular disadvantage (i.e. not being able to be promoted to the top grade) was related to his age.

The case shows that PCPs which disadvantage those who are nearing retirement are very likely to be related to age. For more on retirement, see Chapter 7.

The comparator group should be in materially the same circumstances

In ***Homer***, the employer argued that there was no disadvantage because Mr Homer was in the same position as a younger person without a degree who also had to leave work within a few years, but for family reasons. Lady Hale held that this was the wrong comparison because it equated Mr Homer's disadvantage caused by age, to a similar disadvantage that had nothing to do with age. The circumstances were materially different as Mr Homer did not have a choice about retiring, whereas the younger person could have been more flexible. Her striking analogy was about a woman who argues she is at a disadvantage because of a PCP requiring beards, but then loses her case because the employer argues that there were men who could not grow beards due to illness or immaturity who were at the same disadvantage. This clearly would fly in the face of the aim of the indirect discrimination provisions. In ***Homer***, it also must be relevant that *all* people of Mr Homer's age would not have time to complete a law degree before 65, whereas only *some* younger people would be prevented from completing the degree due to family reasons.

Care therefore needs to be taken to ensure the comparator group is materially in the same situation as the claimant's group. For more on comparators, see Chapter 10.

Establishing a particular disadvantage

The burden is on the claimant to show that the age group or age in question was or would be subject to a particular disadvantage. This will be a matter of evidence. There are some circumstances in which a tribunal may take judicial notice of a particular example of disadvantage – e.g. the fact that women are more likely to have childcare responsibilities than men. In turn this means women will be disproportionately affected by a PCP that makes childcare more difficult. However, these examples are rare and without evidence, a tribunal may not accept a particular disadvantage that may seem obvious to the person experiencing it e.g, that women are more likely to care for older family members.

There are other examples that will be self-evident as a matter of logic. For example, a PCP that a bonus scheme is only applied to those with ten years' work experience is obviously going to disproportionately affect 18-25 year-olds compared to those in their forties.

Statistical evidence

This can be very useful and, whilst not essential, is important to take into account if it exists. However, if statistics exist, they should be considered alongside other evidence rather than in isolation – ***Games v University of Kent*** [2015] IRLR 202. Statistical evidence may not be necessary if the disadvantage is obvious or 'well-recognised' (***Shackletons Garden Centre Ltd v Lowe*** UKEAT/0161/10). In ***Chief Constable of West Yorkshire Police and another v Homer*** [2012] UKSC 15/[2012] ICR 704, SC the Supreme Court noted at para 14 that the way s19 is formulated is intended to '*do away with the need for statistical comparisons where no statistics might exist*'.

In ***Follows v Nationwide Building Society*** ET Case No. 2201937/2018, the claimant cared for her elderly mother and brought a claim based on a PCP that those who did her job role were no longer permitted to work from home. The claim was for both indirect sex and age discrimination on the basis that women and those in their 50s are more likely to have caring responsibilities than men and younger people. The indirect sex discrimination claim succeeded as statistics were available to show that more women than men have caring responsibilities. However, the statistics relating to age did not demonstrate a disadvantage to those in their 50s and for that reason, the claim of indirect age discrimination failed [para 109].

It is sensible therefore to find statistics if they are available. Indeed cases often fail because there is not enough evidence to show a disadvantage to a particular age group. They may be publicly available (in ***Follows*** they were taken from a Carers UK Policy briefing which itself was taken from Office for National Statistics and Census data).

It may also be possible to obtain statistics or information from the employer itself. Although the old statutory procedure for questions under s138 EqA has been repealed, there is nothing to stop a claimant requesting information, as suggested in the explanatory notes to s66 Enterprise and Regulatory Reform Act 2013 (for more on this, see Chapter 8 on Proving age discrimination). In ***Ryan***, the claimant needed to show that the Talent Pool had a disparate effect on older people. The respondent had the statistics so it disclosed them.

An important alternative to statistics may be expert evidence. This may be relevant in cases where the claimant seeks to argue that certain age groups are less capable of certain activities.

<u>There must be a causal link between the PCP and the individual disadvantage</u>

This principle is stated by Lady Hale in ***Essop*** [para 32]. In essence it means that the reason that the group suffers a disadvantage should be the reason the individual suffers the disadvantage. In ***Essop,*** the PCP was a requirement to pass a particular test in order to be promoted. Statistics showed that older and non-white employees were significantly less likely to pass this test than younger people. Nobody knew why this was the case, but this did not matter. A disadvantage to a particular age group was therefore established – members of that age group were less likely to be promoted as they were less likely to pass.

The Supreme Court went on to ask itself about a candidate who was also older and also failed the test meaning she would not be promoted, but failed because of some other reason such as not turning up to the test or not preparing adequately. Lady Hale found that this person would not have suffered harm as a result of the PCP and therefore implied such a claim should not succeed. In other words, the candidate who did not turn up did not fail because of the discriminatory test and so there is no causal link between the fact she failed and the test.

To give another example based on the case of ***Follows*** above, the claimant established that women are more likely to be carers and therefore homeworkers. Homeworkers suffered harm as they were dismissed. She was a homeworker. However, if in fact a colleague was a homeworker because of an unrelated reason (e.g. that she did not like the long commute) then her similar claim may fail unless she could prove that the whole category of homeworkers were also more likely to be women. Without that, the colleague would not have the carers' link to sex.

Not every member of the group has to share the disadvantage

For example, if there is a PCP that 8.30am is a fixed start time, this may disadvantage people in their 30s who are more likely to have children that need to be taken to school. However, clearly not everyone in their 30s has children, it is simply that a higher proportion of that age group does.

Claimant must be put at disadvantage

Establishing a group disadvantage based on statistics is not enough. Section 19(c) EqA 2010 is clear that C has to be put at the disadvantage, either actual or potential. For example, if statistics showed that it was more difficult for older people to pass a test, as in ***Essop***, then an older person who actually passed the test would not be able to bring a claim of indirect discrimination. This may seem very obvious.

However, in the case of ***Keane v Investigo*** UKEAT/0389/09 such a situation was less clear. The claimant, 51, with many years of experience as an accountant, applied for multiple jobs aimed at newly qualified accountants. She was turned down and brought claims against all of the prospective employers. On the face of it, there may have been a PCP which was indirectly discriminatory to those over 50 who were less likely to be newly qualified. However, the tribunal found that she did not really want the jobs but was making a point about the industry and making money out of settlements. The EAT agreed that in her case, she was not subject to any individual disadvantage. This was a question of witness evidence.

In appropriate cases, it may therefore be sensible for respondents not immediately to accept that there must be an individual disadvantage and then cross-examine on this point if necessary.

Examples of particular disadvantage

The following are real examples of particular disadvantage related to age:

- Not being in a pool for promotion (***Ryan***)
- Prevented from being promoted to the top grade of legal adviser (***Homer***)
- Being compulsorily retired (***Harrod***)
- Failing a test for promotion (***Essop***)

'Associative' indirect discrimination

This is a complex area of law without great clarity, unlike the law on *direct* associative discrimination which is more straightforward. Section 13 EqA states that direct discrimination may occur '*because of a protected characteristic.*' A claimant therefore does not have to have a particular protected characteristic in order to claim direct discrimination – if he is treated less favourably because of having a much older partner, he can claim (see Chapter 2 Direct age discrimination). In contrast, s19 EqA is worded such that the individual complaining must have the protected characteristic in question. The concept of associative indirect discrimination grew from European law.

There are arguably two ways of thinking about the idea of associative indirect discrimination. One is when the person is *associated with the PCP* and suffers the same disadvantage but has no connection to the protected characteristic. For example, a policy that employees have to be at work by 9am is likely to indirectly discriminate against women who are more likely to be taking children to school. A man who also cannot arrive at 9am due to childcare would also be disadvantaged under the PCP but would, on the face of it, not be able to claim under s19 EqA 2010 because he does not have the protected characteristic which suffers a group disadvantage.

The second is where a PCP puts a person at a disadvantage because he is *associated with a protected characteristic*. E.g. Robert is 54 years old. He works in a team where everyone else is at least 20 years younger. The employer has a PCP that only those with at least 15 years' experience can deal with the most important clients, which disadvantages the younger members of the team, but not Robert. Robert is entitled to work with the best clients, but because of his association with the team that mostly does not work with the best clients (and is therefore less well-regarded), the best clients do not want to work with him. He is subjected to a detriment because of his association with those who are disadvantaged.

<u>Associated with the PCP – Same disadvantage</u>

Section 19 EqA 2010 does not appear to allow individuals without the protected characteristic but subjected to disadvantage to claim indirect discrimination, but the enactment of s19A EqA 2010 on 1 January 2024 has changed that. The new statute makes clear that someone who is *not* part of the group but nevertheless suffers the same disadvantage can claim. For example, under a PCP that an employee must have ten years of work experience to participate in a bonus scheme, the age group of 18-25 is far more likely than other ages not to have the requisite experience and therefore will be financially disadvantaged. If another employee of 45 in the same company also does not have ten years of experience, not because of youth but because of illness, he can make a claim on the basis that he is suffering the same disadvantage.

In other words, s19A expressly allows the type of associative indirect discrimination where the claimant is associated with the PCP. It reads as follows:

> ***19A Indirect discrimination: same disadvantage***
>
> *(1) A person (A) discriminates against another (B) if—*
>
> *(a) A applies to B a provision, criterion or practice,*
>
> *(b) A also applies, or would apply, the provision, criterion or practice to—*
>
> *(i) persons who share a relevant protected characteristic, and*
>
> *(ii) persons who do not share that relevant protected characteristic,*
>
> *(c) B does not share that relevant protected characteristic,*
>
> *(d) the provision, criterion or practice puts, or would put, persons with the relevant protected characteristic at a particular disadvantage when compared with persons who do not share the relevant protected characteristic,*
>
> *(e) the provision, criterion or practice puts, or would put, B at substantively the same disadvantage as persons who do share the relevant protected characteristic, and*
>
> *(f) A cannot show that the provision, criterion or practice is a proportionate means of achieving a legitimate aim.*

The test is therefore the same as under s19 aside from the fact that the claimant does not need to share the protected characteristic. He essentially piggybacks on another group that is subject to 'classic' indirect discrimination under s19.

In the authors' view, s.19A could be seen as controversial because of the way it widens protection to people without the protected characteristic. Section 19 was introduced to protect those with protected characteristics who would suffer common disadvantage by certain practices. The people protected by s.19A are not in the same group, or even associated with the group which is normally protected. For example, requiring all applicants to be familiar with social media is very likely to disadvantage older applicants. If that rule was not potentially unlawful (subject to justification) under s.19, in effect older people would be excluded from recruitment, leading to inequality and an age disparity in the new recruits. Under s.19A a younger person who is unfamiliar with social media would also be protected. This does not correct an inequality between those with and without a certain protected characteristic. Section 19A is still new and the authors are unaware of any appellate authorities dealing with it. It remains to be seen whether s.19A will be controversial in its application.

Associated with the protected characteristic

Cases are less clear for claimants who suffer because are associated with someone with a protected characteristic, like "Robert" in the fictional example above. Section 19 requires the claimant to have a protected characteristic so would not appear to assist. The Court of Appeal in ***Hainsworth v Ministry of Defence (Equality and Human Rights Commission intervening*** [2014] IRLR 728 did not allow a mother to claim a failure to make reasonable adjustments due to her caring responsibilities for her disabled child.

Trying to use s19A is also not clear. 'Robert' does not share the protected characteristic of those who are disadvantaged (he is not younger) but he doesn't share the same disadvantage either, because he is permitted to work with the most important clients. On the face of it, he will not satisfy the test.

However, the answer may well be to reframe the claim. Rather than identifying the PCP as not being allowed to work with the best clients without significant experience, and the disadvantage as being that clients did not want to work with him due to his association with the younger team, Robert could argue, under s19A, that the disadvantage caused by the PCP is a lack of promotion / pay-rise due to being less well-regarded. Robert would then be able to claim under s.19A that he shared the disadvantage of the younger people being less well-regarded and less likely to be promoted.

The only other way to argue such a point would be to refer to ECJ jurisprudence (which is now more difficult since Brexit), and in particular the case of ***CHEZ Razpredelenie Bulgaria AD v Komisia za zashtita ot diskriminatsia*** [2015] EUECJ C-83/14, CJEU. The claimant lived in a mainly Roma area where the authorities had put electricity meters 6-7 metres high off the ground to prevent tampering. She succeeded in her argument that the authorities were discriminating against Roma people (whom they assumed would tamper) and that she also suffered the disadvantage of finding it difficult to access her meter.

CHEZ is clearly a same disadvantage case because the difficulty with accessing the meter applied to the Roma group and also to her. The ECJ were express about this. She was however arguably also associated with the protected characteristic because she lived in a Roma area. Advocate General Kokott suggested in her opinion [AG107] the possibility of indirect discrimination due to association with a protected characteristic. Although this was not adopted by the Grand Chamber, it may open the door to the second type of indirect associative discrimination in the future.

The ET case of ***Follows v Nationwide Building Society*** [2023] UKET 2201937/2018, referred to CHEZ. The tribunal decided that Mrs Follows had been subject to indirect associative disability discrimination (due to her status as a carer for her disabled mother) as homeworking posts had been deleted.

That case was decided before s19A came into force which arguably indicates that Parliament intended to restrict the ambit of indirect associative discrimination to the first category – i.e. *same disadvantage* cases. If at all possible, a claim should therefore be framed with s19A in mind, thereby avoiding the numerous hurdles of relying on European law.

CHAPTER FOUR

JUSTIFICATION

- *What was the employer aiming to do by treating the worker in a discriminatory way?*
- *Was that a legitimate aim, in other words, a real, appropriate, objective consideration?*
- *In a direct discrimination complaint, would the legitimate aim also assist society in some way?*
- *If so, was it a proportionate way of achieving that aim or could a less discriminatory measure have achieved the same result?*

In both direct and indirect age discrimination claims, it is possible for the respondent to argue that the less favourable treatment because of age or the provision, criterion or practice ("PCP") which disadvantages people of a certain age, is objectively justifiable and therefore not unlawful. Direct age discrimination is the only form of direct discrimination which can permissibly be justified.

Once a tribunal is satisfied that there has been less favourable treatment because of age, or a PCP which disadvantages people of a certain age, it is for the employer to show that this is justified. It is not an easy task. The tribunal will scrutinise the evidence to ensure that the employer has not gone too far in trying to achieve a certain aim because the employer is only permitted to go as far as is reasonable and necessary to achieve the aim in question.

What are the statutory tests?

Section 13 of the EqA relevantly states:

13 Direct discrimination

(1) A person (A) discriminates against another (B) if, because of a protected characteristic, A treats B less favourably than A treats or would treat others.

(2) If the protected characteristic is age, A does not discriminate against B if A can show A's treatment of B to be a proportionate means of achieving a legitimate aim.

Section 19 of the EqA relevantly states:

19 Indirect discrimination

(1) A person (A) discriminates against another (B) if A applies to B a provision, criterion or practice which is discriminatory in relation to a relevant protected characteristic of B's.

(2) For the purposes of subsection (1), a provision, criterion or practice is discriminatory in relation to a relevant protected characteristic of B's if—

(a) A applies, or would apply, it to persons with whom B does not share the characteristic,

(b) it puts, or would put, persons with whom B shares the characteristic at a particular disadvantage when compared with persons with whom B does not share it,

(c) it puts, or would put, B at that disadvantage, and

(d) A cannot show it to be a proportionate means of achieving a legitimate aim.

Key points

In ***Bilka-Kaufhaus GmbH v Weber von Hartz*** [1987] ICR 110, the ECJ analysed the application of the European justification test contained in art 2 of the EU Equal Treatment Framework Directive 2000/78/EC, which states the measure is discriminatory unless it is *'objectively justified by a legitimate aim and the means of achieving that aim are appropriate and necessary'*. To justify an objective with discriminatory effect, the ECJ found that an employer must show that the means chosen for achieving that objective:

1. correspond to a real need on the part of the undertaking;

2. are appropriate with a view to achieving the objective in question; and

3. are necessary to that end.

According to Lady Hale in ***Homer v Chief Constable of West Yorkshire Police and West Yorkshire Police Authority*** [2012] UKSC 15, at paragraph 22:

> *'Although the [UK legislation] refers only to a 'proportionate means of achieving a legitimate aim', this has to be read in the light of the Directive which it implements. To be proportionate, a measure has to be both an appropriate means of achieving the legitimate aim and (reasonably) necessary in order to do so'.*

The burden of proof is firmly on the respondent to establish justification: see ***Starmer v British Airways*** [2005] IRLR 862 at [31]. Once the less favourable treatment has been established as being because of age, or the practice in question has been found to have had the requisite disparate effect on people of a certain age, if the respondent does not manage to demonstrate that the treatment or measure in question was a proportionate means of achieving a legitimate aim, the claim of discrimination will succeed.

The Employment Equality (Repeal of Retirement Age Provisions) Regulations 2011, SI 2011/1069 repealed the exceptions to direct age discrimination related to default retirement age. This means that an employer must now objectively justify any retirement age (see Chapter 7 Retirement). There are some preserved exceptions to age discrimination contained in those and other Regulations, which are outside the scope of this book.

Is justifying direct age discrimination different to justifying indirect age discrimination?

The words used in both sections 13 and 19 of EqA are identical, but it is clear that it is more difficult for an employer to justify direct discrimination than indirect discrimination. The Supreme Court in ***Seldon v Clarkson Wright and Jakes (and Secretary of State for Business Innovation and Skills, and Age UK – Intervenors)*** [2012] UKSC 16, [2012] IRLR 590, applied the relevant European case law to a case involving a mandatory retirement age for a partner in a law firm. Lady Hale held that the approach to justification of direct age discrimination is '*significantly different*' to justification of indirect discrimination. Direct discrimination – such as mandatory retirement – may only be justified if the relevant treatment or provision seeks to achieve a legitimate aim of a public interest nature related to employment policy, the labour market and vocational training. A distinction had to be drawn between those types of social policy objectives, and purely individual reasons that are specific to the situation of a particular employer such as cost reduction or improving competitiveness, which could not justify direct discrimination.

What is a legitimate aim?

There is no definitive, exhaustive list of aims which will be upheld as legitimate. It will be a matter of judgment for the tribunal in any particular case. It is clear that the aim must reflect a genuine need of the business in question and must not be discriminatory in itself. The EHRC Code mentions that the health, welfare and safety of individuals may qualify as a legitimate aim (see para 4.28). This might cover, for example, the imposition of health checks or medical requirements that potentially discriminate against older workers.

The EAT in ***National Union of Rail, Maritime and Transport Workers v Lloyd*** [2019] IRLR 897, upheld the tribunal's finding that a trade union was unable to rely on "*intergenerational fairness*" as its legitimate aim for refusing a 62-year-old member to stand for election to its National Executive Committee. The EAT provided guidance on the best approach to dealing with a legitimate aim in a structured way by answering the following questions in sequence: (a) whether each asserted aim was a true aim and actual objective; (b) whether it was capable of being a legitimate aim; and (c) whether it was a legitimate aim in the particular circumstances. This case also demonstrates that commonly accepted legitimate aims such as intergenerational fairness will not automatically be waved through and will be subject to scrutiny on a case-by-case basis.

Although it is necessary for the aim to be a genuine and true aim of the respondent, it need not have been articulated or even realised at the time the measure was first adopted – it could provide rationalisation retrospectively (***Cadman v Health & Safety Executive*** [2004] IRLR 971, as confirmed by the Supreme Court in ***Seldon v Clarkson Wright and Jakes*** (as above)).

Appellate courts have repeatedly cautioned against the imposition of a requirement for concrete evidence to be adduced in relation to every assertion (related to legitimate aims or proportionality) to justify a particular measure. Common sense and reasonable and rational argument can sometimes be sufficient, though subjective impression, mere generalisations or stereotyped assumptions must be avoided (see the judgment of Elias P, as he then was, at EAT level in ***Seldon v Clarkson Wright and Jakes*** [2009] IRLR 267, and the EAT in ***Chief Constable of West Yorkshire Police and West Yorkshire Police Authority v Homer*** [2009] IRLR 262). An employer seeking to rely on a legitimate aim would nevertheless be well-advised to adduce evidence in relation to it, to demonstrate, in particular, the genuine need for the objective in question, and whether it was a legitimate aim in the particular circumstances (see ***Hardy & Hansons plc v Lax*** [2005] IRLR 726, paras 31-32). In the recent employment tribunal decision of ***Scott v Walker Morris LLP*** ET Case no. 1806503/2023, L.S.G. 2025, 122(8), the tribunal found that the aim of intergenerational fairness was legitimate, but the law firm respondent did not adduce sufficient evidence to support a conclusion that "*forcing*" retirement at age 63 was necessary for workforce and succession planning. Had there been evidence of senior partners "*hogging the equity*" or of the firm needing to free up equity for younger partners, the result on justification might have been different.

Similarly, in ***Hannell v Rydon Group Ltd*** ET Case No.2376701/11, the tribunal decided that using "*experience*" as a selection criterion in a redundancy exercise was not justified. The employer had brought no evidence to demonstrate why the use of such a criterion was a proportionate means of achieving a legitimate aim, so was found to have indirectly discriminated against the younger candidate for redundancy who could not compete with the older employee who had considerably more experience in a particular project.

Is the PCP / treatment in question appropriate to achieve the aim?

Once a legitimate aim has been identified and shown to be a genuine aim of the employer, the tribunal will then need to consider whether the PCP or treatment in question in fact achieves that aim. That will require evidence to be presented by the respondent.

The EAT considered justification recently in the EAT in ***Fasano v Reckitt Benkiser Group*** [2024] EAT 7 (31 January 2024, unreported). Judge Shanks found that, where a provision, criterion or practice (PCP) is in issue, it is important that any justification relates directly to that PCP, not to other matters more generally. The tribunal had dismissed the indirect age discrimination claim of a senior employee who had left his employment in June 2019, being a "good leaver" for the purposes of a Long Term Incentive Plan (LTIP). Under the LTIP he was entitled to a pro-rated amount of the 2017 award which would ordinarily vest at the end of 2019. As a result of the performance of certain shares in 2019, it became clear that the 2017 awards would not vest in 2019. In September 2019, it was decided that the terms of the 2017 award would be changed so part of it would vest in 2019, notwithstanding the poor performance, with the aim of retaining existing employees, who would otherwise receive nothing in respect of the 2017 award. A condition of the award was that the employee was still employed in September 2019 (which the claimant was not). The employee complained that the PCP of requiring employees to be employed in September 2019 to benefit from the scheme-change, put him, and employees older than 57 (who were more likely to have retired before September 2019), at a disadvantage and was therefore indirect age discrimination. The tribunal found that the cut-off date requiring employees to be in employment was a proportionate means of achieving the legitimate aim of incentivising senior staff to remain in employment. Judge Shanks disagreed, saying (at paragraphs 14 and 16):

> "*The change to the performance criteria and the vesting date for the awards both contributed to the legitimate aim of retention but it was the specific PCP and not the changes as a whole that needed to be justified... Even if it was thought that there was a need for "some sort of qualifying or cut off date" in relation to the amended performance condition, the relevant PCP could not contribute to retention of staff... (T)he only real justification for the PCP was to avoid unnecessary payments to those who could not be retained, ie to save the expenditure of money. But it was never part of the Respondents' case that the legitimate aim of the PCP was to save money or that they could not afford to pay the participants in the 2017 LTIP award who had left before 18 September 2019 what would otherwise become due to them.*
>
> *I fully accept that the legitimate aim of the changes to the performance criteria under the LTIP was to retain staff who might otherwise leave before May 2020 and that payments to Mr Fasano and the other 23 would not assist in this aim. But this is no answer*

> *to the claim for indirect age discrimination. The Respondents chose to use the changes to the LTIP as a means of achieving their aim of retaining staff rather than, for example, introducing a free-standing scheme involving straightforward "retention payments" to existing staff. As part of those changes, they introduced a PCP which did not itself contribute to the achievement of the aim at all. It was necessary to justify that PCP, not the overall changes to the LTIP."*

In other words, the company could have incentivised the same people to stay in employment without excluding from payment the people who were no longer in employment. The company, therefore needed to focus on justifying the PCP of *not* paying people who were no longer employed by September 2019, instead of focusing on the aim of the whole scheme of rewarding those who had remained employed.

The focus must also be on whether the aim which the Respondent was actually pursuing was legitimate, not whether the tribunal considers that the Respondent should have been pursuing different aims, which would have had a less discriminatory impact. In ***HM Land Registry v Benson and others*** [2012] ICR 627, the tribunal were found to have failed to assess the means to achieve the employer's aims but instead had assessed the means to achieve a different aim, thereby impermissibly substituting its judgment in a commercial decision. That case concerned an employer who applied a "cheapness criterion" when deciding which employees could take advantage of an early retirement scheme. That criterion placed those aged 50-54 years old at a particular disadvantage because they were the most expensive employees who were entitled to take early retirement, and were therefore not selected for the scheme. The EAT found that reducing headcount was a legitimate aim and the cheapness criterion was a proportionate and practical means of achieving that aim. The decision of the tribunal was therefore overturned because the tribunal found that the employer could have afforded not to reduce headcount and therefore it was not justifiable to have that aim. That was the wrong approach because the tribunal had not scrutinised the means of achieving the legitimate aim of the employer.

It is also important that the aim itself is not discriminatory. The Court of Appeal in ***Allonby v Accrington and Rossendale College and ors*** [2001] ICR 1189 found that, where a college had dismissed all part-time lecturers to avoid paying them certain statutory benefits, the aim was unlawful and sex discriminatory and therefore could not be upheld as legitimate. In an age discrimination context, for example, where a gym owner moves the younger employees to front-of-house duties, and the older employees have to do harder work behind the scenes, with the employer's aim being to create a public image of being young, fit and dynamic, that aim is discriminatory in itself and cannot be used to justify the practice.

Cost

Can the aim of saving cost be legitimate, for the purpose of justifying age discrimination? Of course, it is not particularly palatable for employers to be allowed to discriminate against their employees because it would be cheaper to do so than to avoid discriminating, but there are some circumstances in which employers have sought to justify discrimination on costs grounds, and have succeeded. The ECJ has made clear that cost will not be a legitimate aim to justify direct discrimination, though budgetary consideration can underpin the social policy of a Member State which is legitimate (see ***Fuchs and Köhler v Land Hessen: C-159/10 and C-160/10*** [2011] IRLR 1043).

It is now well established that saving cost cannot be the only aim of an indirectly discriminatory provision, criterion or practice ("PCP") to be justifiable. It can, however, be cited by an employer as one of a number of factors justifying indirect discrimination. This has become known as "*cost plus*", though that is not a label of which the higher courts have consistently approved.

In ***Cross and ors v British Airways plc*** [2005] IRLR 423, EAT (a sex discrimination case) the EAT found that an employer cannot solely rely on considerations of cost to justify a discriminatory provision, but may be permitted to put cost into the balance together with other justifications, if there are any. In ***Benson*** (as above), the EAT found that the aims of the employer were to reduce headcount in such a way that its costs did not exceed its revenue, or to reduce the number of applicants at a cost which came within the £12 million budget. Seeking to break even and allocating resources appropriately were found to be legitimate aims. Although reducing cost was part of those legitimate aims, cost was not the sole criterion. The EAT noted that imposing a "maximum spend" was not inherently discriminatory against particular age groups, but the discriminatory impact was as a result of the particular selection criterion chosen rather than the aim pursued.

The Court of Appeal in ***Woodcock v Cumbria Primary Care Trust*** [2012] IRLR 491 put to rest some of the speculation caused by comments of the then President of the EAT, Underhill P, in the EAT in that case ([2011] IRLR 119). Underhill P had expressed some doubt that reducing cost could never be a legitimate aim in isolation, but Lord Justice Rimer made clear, dismissing the claim of indirect age discrimination, that,

> *"the guidance of the Court of Justice is that an employer cannot justify discriminatory treatment "solely" because the elimination of such treatment would involve increased costs. This means no more than that the saving or avoidance of costs will not, without more, amount to the achieving of a legitimate aim".*

In ***Woodcock,*** the respondent employer was found to be justified in making the claimant redundant just before the age he would have been eligible for early retirement. The aims, found to be legitimate, were twofold: (1) to save the substantial cost it would otherwise have incurred in funding his early retirement; and (2) to avoid the claimant receiving an unexpected windfall (he could have been made redundant long previously if the employer had not been very slow in carrying out its redundancy procedure).

Similarly, the tribunal in ***Braithwaite v HCL Insurance BPO*** [2015] ICR 713 dismissed a claim for indirect discrimination where the employer sought to address continuing losses by requiring their employees to agree to certain terms and conditions or be dismissed. That requirement put older employees at a particular disadvantage as employees within the 38 to 64 year age range were more likely to lose their existing contractual rights. The tribunal found that the requirement to enter a new contract was a provision, criterion or practice ("PCP") but also held, however, that the PCP was objectively justified. The EAT upheld the legitimate aims of reducing staff costs to ensure the employer's future viability and to have in place a market competitive, non-discriminatory set of terms and conditions, although the appeal was not brought on the basis of the "*cost plus*" principle. This case illustrates an argument that "*balancing the books*" is not an aim which is only concerned with cost, and therefore potentially is legitimate.

Lord Justice Underhill in ***Heskett v Secretary of State for Justice*** [2021] IRLR 132, CA, made clear that where "*the employer's aim in acting in the way that gives rise to the discriminatory impact can fairly be described as no more than a wish to save costs*" that can never be justifiable. Underhill LJ did, however, expressly disapprove of the label of "*cost plus*" because, he said, it encouraged "*an inappropriately mechanistic approach*". At paragraph 89 he stated:

> *"It is better, in any case where the issue arises, to consider how the employer's aim can most fairly be characterised, looking at the total picture. It is only if the fair characterisation is indeed that the aim was solely to avoid increased costs that it has to be treated as illegitimate."*

The mechanistic approach criticised by Underhill LJ has meant that lawyers, understandably perhaps, will look for another justification, even if it is rather weak and artificial, in addition to cost, so they can try to persuade a judge that it is "*cost plus*". An illustration of the thin line between an illegitimate aim solely to save cost, and a legitimate "*cost plus*" rationale can be seen in comparing the ***Woodcock*** case (as above) with ***Cook v Gentoo Group Ltd*** [2023] IRLR 357, EAT. Both cases were factually similar, except that, in ***Woodcock*** the redundancy process had taken a long time due to delays on the part of the employer, and could have been concluded considerably before the early retirement date, whereas the employer in ***Cook*** abbreviated the normal process to ensure that the employee did not reach retirement age before the redundancy took effect. Both employers' stated aims included to avoid a windfall for the claimant. In ***Cook,*** the EAT found that a fair characterisation of the aim was solely to save costs, and was therefore not legitimate and the discriminatory measure not justified, contrary to ***Woodcock***.

This will continue to be a tricky area for employment lawyers. Considerable thought will need to be given to the genuine aims of the employer and whether, in fact, cost-saving is the only aim of implementing a certain measure, in reality.

Social policy aims in direct (and indirect) age discrimination cases

In broad terms, Lady Hale in ***Seldon*** categorised legitimate social policy objectives in direct age discrimination cases, as either: "*intergenerational fairness*" or "*dignity*". Lady Hale's comments have been incorporated into a supplement to the EHRC Code on Employment (dated March 2014), at paragraph 3.4.2, where legitimate aims are listed as including:

- promoting access to employment for younger people
- the efficient planning of the departure and recruitment of staff
- sharing out employment opportunities fairly between the generations
- ensuring the mix of generations of staff so as to promote the exchange of experience and new ideas
- rewarding experience
- cushioning the blow for long-serving employees who may find it hard to find new employment if dismissed
- facilitating the participation of older workers in the workforce.

Lady Hale in ***Seldon*** also mentioned (at paragraph 50): (1) avoiding the need to dismiss employees on the ground that they are no longer capable of doing the job which may be humiliating for the employee concerned; or (2) avoiding disputes about the employee's fitness for work over a certain age.

Lady Hale additionally made clear that it is not enough to show that an aim falls within a category of legitimate aims; it must be established that the aim is legitimate in the particular circumstances of the employment concerned. She gave two examples. First was the aim of improving the recruitment of young people in order to achieve a balanced and diverse workforce. "*This is in principle a legitimate aim. But if there is in fact no problem in recruiting the young and the problem is in retaining the older and more experienced workers then it may not be a legitimate aim for the business concerned.*" Her second example was the aim of avoiding the need for performance management. This may be a legitimate aim, but if in fact the business already has sophisticated performance management measures in place, it may not be legitimate to avoid them for only one section of the workforce.

In the context of seeking to justify direct age discrimination on social or labour policy grounds, the ECJ said in ***R (on the application of Age UK) v Secretary of State for Business, Innovation and Skills*** [2009] IRLR 1017 (at [51]):

> *"mere generalisations concerning the capacity of a specific measure to contribute to employment policy, labour market or vocational training objectives are not enough . . . and do not constitute evidence on the basis of which it could reasonably be considered that the means chosen are suitable for achieving that aim."*

An example of an upheld legitimate aim related to intergenerational fairness is in ***Air Products plc v Cockram*** [2018] IRLR 755, CA. This concerned an employer increasing its customary retirement age from 50 to 55, with the effect that the claimant could not access unvested awards under a long-term investment plan when he retired aged 50, whereas a hypothetical comparator retiring at 55 years old (or older) would be able to access such awards. Before the employment tribunal, it was agreed that the effect of the customary retirement age provision in the investment plan was directly discriminatory. However, the tribunal accepted that the discriminatory effect was objectively justified on the basis that the employer wished to achieve intergenerational fairness and consistency, reward experience and loyalty, and ensure a mix of generations of staff. It held that applying the retirement exception only to employees over 55 was a proportionate means of achieving a legitimate aim.

Legitimate aims in indirect age discrimination

As stated above, the range of aims which could be upheld as legitimate in indirect discrimination claims is wider than in direct discrimination claims. Social policy aims can potentially justify both direct and indirect discrimination, but other aims can also justify indirectly discriminatory measures. The aims do not have to be in the public interest in the same way, but the aims of measures which have a disparate effect on people of certain ages will still be scrutinised to ensure they are legitimate and genuine.

The tribunal will bear in mind that, however laudable an aim might be, it still must be a genuine aim of the business, related to its needs in discharging its function – see ***Greater Manchester Police Authority v Lea*** [1990] IRLR 372, EAT. In that case, the employer sought to justify a policy of excluding those holding an occupational pension from consideration for a job by reference to the social aim of providing employment for individuals with no other source of income. Given that there was no link between the functional needs of the employer and the imposition of the PCP, the aim could not justify the PCP.

As an example of three objectives that have been held capable of being legitimate aims in an age discrimination case, the EAT upheld in ***MacCulloch v ICI plc*** [2008] IRLR 846 (a) rewarding loyalty; (b) protecting older workers because they were more vulnerable in the job market; and (c) encouraging older workers to leave in order to create space for younger ones. The employer had a redundancy payments scheme under which the size of the payments increased with age and length of service. Interestingly, Mr Justice Elias, President of the EAT as he then was, considered that, as regards the employer's aim of helping older employees who are particularly vulnerable in the job market, it was not necessary for the employer to produce evidence that older workers find it harder to obtain work than younger workers, since the tribunal had been fully entitled to draw on its own experience in this respect.

The case of ***Homer v Chief Constable of West Yorkshire Police and West Yorkshire Police Authority*** [2012] IRLR 601 concerned a requirement to hold a degree before being eligible for a top band of pay, which was found by the Supreme Court to be unjustifiable age discrimination. The Chief Constable argued that the requirement was a proportionate means of achieving the legitimate aim of facilitating the recruitment of suitable staff. The aim was held to be legitimate, but the requirement was said to be disproportionate.

Other well-known legitimate aims that could justify indirect age discrimination include:

(1) operational integrity;

(2) health and safety;

(3) client needs;

(4) corporate image; and

(5) promoting equal opportunities.

Proportionality

The principle of proportionality requires the tribunal to strike an objective balance between the discriminatory effect of the treatment / PCP and the reasonable needs of the employer's business. There is no guidance in the EqA about this, and it is for the tribunal to assess proportionality.

Lord Justice Sedley in ***Allonby v Accrington and Rossendale College and ors*** (a sex discrimination case, as above) set out the responsibility of the tribunal to scrutinise the alleged business needs put forward by the employer to justify indirect sex discrimination. Once a finding of discriminatory treatment or a PCP having a disparate and adverse impact on people with a certain protected characteristic (such as people of a certain age) had been made, and where the treatment in question was a dismissal,

> *"what was required was at the minimum a critical evaluation of whether the [employer]'s reasons demonstrated a real need to dismiss the applicant; if there was such a need, consideration of the seriousness of the disparate impact of the [PCP] on women including the applicant; and an evaluation of whether the former were sufficient to outweigh the latter.'*

The ACAS Guidance "*Age discrimination: key points for the workplace*" (February 2019, most recently updated in April 2024) describes (p.20) the obligation on the employer to act proportionately thus:

> *"To justify this sort of action, an employer must balance its business need against the discriminatory effect on affected employees. The more discriminatory the effect, the more difficult it will be to justify. Employers should explore ways to achieve their aims without discriminating, or without discriminating as much. If there are less discriminatory alternatives, they should be taken".*

Just like proving a legitimate aim, there is no absolute requirement for evidence to be adduced to prove that the measure was proportionate, as the ET can rely on common sense, or rational argument to find that the PCP or treatment was a proportionate means of achieving the aim. Sometimes, as discussed in ***Cockram*** (above), the treatment will so obviously be proportionate that it barely requires any evidence at all.

Parties would nevertheless be well-advised to consider what evidence they can bring to the tribunal to demonstrate that their treatment or PCP was proportionate to achieve the aim.

Was the treatment appropriate to achieve the aim?

The real question is not whether the treatment is appropriate – there does not seem to be a definition or explanation of what "appropriate" really means in this context. Instead, tribunals tend to ask whether the treatment is not inappropriate and not inherently discriminatory. Lady Hale in ***Chief Constable of West Yorkshire Police and another v Homer*** (above) (at paragraph 22) gave some useful examples of what measures would be considered inappropriate:

> *"Some measures may simply be inappropriate to the aim in question: thus, for example, the aim of rewarding experience is not achieved by age related pay scales which apply irrespective of experience (**Hennigs v Eisenbahn-Bundesamt** (Joined Cases C-297/10 and C-298/10) [2012] 1 CMLR 484); the aim of making it easier to recruit young people is not achieved by a measure which applies long after the employees have ceased to be young (**Kücükdeveci v Swedex GmbH & Co KG** (Case C-555/07) [2011] 2 CMLR 703).*

If the means used to achieve a legitimate aim are found to have been manipulative, they are unlikely to be considered proportionate (***GMB v Allen and ors*** [2008] ICR 1407, CA).

Was the treatment reasonably necessary?

Although the ECJ in ***Bilka-Kaufhaus GmbH v Weber von Hartz*** [1987] ICR 110, found that a measure is *"objectively justified by a legitimate aim (when) the means of achieving that aim are appropriate and necessary"*, it has subsequently been emphasised that the reference to "*necessary*" means *"reasonably necessary"*: see ***Rainey v Greater Glasgow Health Board*** (HL) [1987] IRLR 26 per Lord Keith of Kinkel at pp.30–31. In other words, the employer does not have to go so far as to prove that the only way a legitimate aim could be achieved is by the treatment / PCP in question. As the EHRC Code puts it (at paragraph 4.31) "*it is sufficient that the same aim could not be achieved by less discriminatory means*".

In ***HM Land Registry v Benson and ors*** [2012] ICR 627 (discussed above), the tribunal found that because the extra cost of not implementing the discriminatory measure was "not unaffordable", meaning that the employer would not have been made insolvent if forced to pay it, the discriminatory measure was disproportionate. The tribunal found that the employer did not have a "real need" to keep within a certain budget. The EAT found this was the wrong approach, elevating the requirement to the means having to be the only way of achieving the aim – absolute necessity – rather than being "*reasonably necessary*".

Although assessing whether the treatment / PCP was reasonably necessary is not to be conflated with the range of reasonable responses test, tribunals have been encouraged by the EAT to give a substantial degree of respect to the judgment of the employer as to what is reasonably necessary to achieve a legitimate aim – see ***Birtenshaw v Oldfield*** [2019] IRLR 946.

On remittal from the Supreme Court, the law firm respondent in ***Seldon v Clarkson Wright and Jakes (No.2)*** [2014] ICR 1275, EAT, sought to justify the default retirement age ("DRA") of partners of 65 and relied upon the legitimate aims of facilitating employee retention and succession planning. Evidence was presented that more junior employees, if required to wait longer for promotion, might seek opportunities elsewhere; but if the DRA was too low, there might be concern about how long one would spend in the partnership. The EAT found that only a narrow range of ages met these criteria. Mr Seldon argued that a retirement age of 68 or 70 would have worked just as well and therefore a DRA of 68 or over was a less discriminatory way of achieving the same aim. The EAT considered the following factors in deciding that the choice of a DRA of 65 was proportionate: (a) the partners all consented to the choice of 65 in the partnership deed; (b) the statutory default retirement age (since repealed) at the time was 65; (c) the state pension age for men at the time was 65; and (d) the ECJ had upheld 65 as a retirement age for a variety of different aims. The EAT noted that the issue for the tribunal was to determine where the balance lay between the discriminatory effect of choosing a particular age and its success in achieving the employer's legitimate aim. That balance, like any balance, will not necessarily show that a particular point can be identified as being any more or less appropriate than another point. Given the realities of setting any particular bright line date, the tribunal was required to consider what was reasonably necessary to achieve the aims. The fact that it was possible to identify a range of ages which could have achieved the aims did not mean that the employer could justify only the highest age in the range. For more analysis of ***Seldon***, see Chapter 7 Retirement.

It is fair, therefore, to say that even if the tribunal could conceive of a less discriminatory measure which could achieve the same aim, that is not necessarily the death knell of a justification defence, as long as the respondent can persuade a tribunal that the measure was nevertheless reasonably necessary. Claimants would be well advised to describe, and adduce evidence to demonstrate to the tribunal, that a less discriminatory measure could achieve the same aim, in order to undermine the respondent's arguments on whether the treatment complained of was reasonably necessary.

In ***Homer,*** the Supreme Court found it should ask itself whether "*requiring existing employees to have a law degree before they could achieve the higher threshold is appropriate to the aims of recruiting and retaining new staff or retaining existing staff within the organisation.*" It also had to be asked whether "*it was reasonably necessary in order to achieve the legitimate aims of the scheme to deny those benefits*" to people in the claimant's position (paras 22 and 24). The Supreme Court found that the requirement was neither appropriate to the aims nor reasonably necessary and was not therefore justified.

The tribunal decision in ***Baker v National Air Traffic Services Ltd*** ET Case No 220350107 (24 February 2009, unreported) provides an example where the tribunal followed the formula set out in ***Homer*** to find that the treatment was not justified. The respondent operated a directly discriminatory age bar, refusing to accept any applicants over the age of 35 for the post of air traffic controller. The respondent relied upon aims including maximising success in training and a reasonable period of service after qualification and adduced expert evidence to support the proposition that cognitive ability declines with age, and therefore younger applicants were more likely to succeed in training. The aims were held to be legitimate and related to or connected to a business need – reasonableness did not play a part at that stage. The tribunal were not, however, impressed with the expert evidence and found that the treatment did not achieve the aims. The tribunal's conclusion was that the needs of the business did not outweigh the discriminatory effect. Furthermore, the tribunal considered that there were appropriate alternatives to the age bar which would have satisfied the aims, which were available. Justification for the age bar was not therefore made out.

The two decisions of the ECJ in ***Wolf v Stadt Frankfurt am Main*** C-229/08 [2010] IRLR 244, and ***Vital Pérez v Ayuntamiento De Oviedo*** C-416/14 [2015] IRLR 158 dealt with the same age bar of 30 for recruitment into the fire service (in ***Wolf***) and a local police force (***Vital Pérez***). The court found that there was a genuine occupational requirement/legitimate aims of ensuring particular physical capabilities were maintained for the operational capacity and/or proper functioning of the service, but in ***Wolf*** the age-bar was found to be proportionate, whereas in ***Vital Pérez*** it was not. Not all the capacities local police officers needed to possess were found to be comparable to the exceptionally high physical capacities regularly required by firefighters.

The Court of Appeal, in ***Rolls Royce v Unite*** [2009] IRLR 576, considered that use of the renowned "last-in, first out" ("LIFO") criterion for redundancy selection was justified, notwithstanding its indirectly discriminatory effect on the younger employees. The legitimate aims were identified as the reward of loyalty, and the overall desirability of achieving a stable workforce in the context of a fair process of redundancy selection. The Court of Appeal found that it was proportionate to include consideration of length of service where it was one of a number of selection criteria used. Although there was some criticism of the Court of

Appeal's approach to jurisdiction in the ***Rolls Royce*** case – see ***National Union of Rail, Maritime and Transport Workers and anor v Tyne and Wear Passenger Transport Executive t/a Nexus*** [2024] UKSC 37, SC – the principle in relation to LIFO being justified in these circumstances is likely to stand.

Balancing the employer's need against the discriminatory effect

In general, the greater the disadvantage caused by the treatment/PCP, the more cogent the justification that is needed – ***Hardy & Hansons plc v Lax*** [2005] IRLR 726. The assessment of proportionality involves balancing the benefit of the aim sought by the employer and the impact on the adversely affected group – ***CHEZ Razpredelenie Bulgaria AD v Komisia za zashtita ot diskriminatsia*** C-83/14, [2015] IRLR, ECJ.

The balancing exercise was considered by the House of Lords in ***Barry v Midland Bank plc*** [1999] ICR 859 which was a sex discrimination case. The ground being relied upon as justification was said to need to be "*of sufficient importance for the national court to regard this as overriding the disparate impact of the difference in treatment, either in whole or in part. The more serious the disparate impact on women, or men as the case may be, the more cogent must be the objective justification.*" This suggests that, in an age discrimination case, not only would directly discriminatory treatment be more difficult to justify, but an indirectly discriminatory PCP which had a high degree of disparate impact would require particularly stringent scrutiny of the arguments about proportionality.

When weighing the discriminatory effect of the PCP (or treatment) the tribunal should not focus on the claimant's level of upset in their particular circumstances but on the impact of the PCP on the group (who share the protected characteristic) generally (***NSL Ltd v Zaluski*** [2024] EAT 86).

CHAPTER FIVE

HARASSMENT RELATED TO AGE

- *Has the claimant experienced unwanted conduct?*
- *Did the unwanted conduct have the proscribed purpose or effect?*
- *Was the unwanted conduct related to the protected characteristic of age?*

Section 26 of the Equality Act 2010 ('EqA') protects individuals from harassment. Under section 26, three forms of behaviour are prohibited. However, the only one relevant to the protected characteristic of age is set out under section 26(1).

Under section 26(1), harassment is defined as: "*Unwanted conduct related to a relevant protected characteristic*" which has the "*purpose of effect of (i) violating [a person's dignity, or (ii) creating an intimidating, hostile, degrading, humiliating or offensive environment*" for that person. This chapter looks at what is necessary to prove claims of age-related harassment and difficulties that can arise when establishing whether "*banter*" or other commentary is sufficiently serious to be considered harassment.

Facts that give rise to a harassment claim cannot also give rise to a claim of victimisation or direct discrimination. Section 212(1) EqA and the accompanying Explanatory Notes make clear that a "*detriment*" cannot be conduct that is also considered harassment. Harassment and direct discrimination claims are therefore mutually exclusive, assuming they arise from the same factual allegation. For this reason, harassment claims are often run in the alternative to direct discrimination claims. As will be explored in this chapter, unlike direct discrimination claims, when bringing claims of harassment, claimants do not have to concern themselves with identifying a comparator, either real or hypothetical, or with proving that something happened "*because of*" the protected characteristic of age.

Unwanted conduct

The first question for the tribunal will be whether there was unwanted conduct.

"*Conduct*" covers a wide spectrum of behaviour from actions to oral and written statements. As was made clear in ***Driscoll v V&P Global Ltd*** [2021] 7 WLUK 206, a dismissal, including a constructive dismissal, can also amount to "*conduct*" under section 26.

"*Unwanted*" conduct is not a term of art. If remarks or behaviour are unwelcome or uninvited, they will be considered "*unwanted*" (***Insitu Cleaning Co Ltd v Heads*** [1994] 8 WLUK 138). However, it must be conduct that was unwanted to the claimant, not conduct that might be considered objectively unwanted in general by the Tribunal.

Although conduct must be considered from the claimant's perspective, that does not mean that the claimant must be present when the conduct takes place or that the conduct needs to be addressed to the claimant.

An example of this is ***Mason v AG Parfett and Sons Ltd*** ET Case No.2401747/14 (unreported). In ***Mason***, the claimant, a general manager, had been heavily criticised in a managers' meeting, in part for being uninterested in both a revamp project and in the development of younger employees. Shortly after this, a director of the company was interviewed for a trade magazine. In the interview, the manager said that he was frustrated by "*some people's inability to move on, adapt to change and develop the next generation. I realise that resistance to change and modernity, in work or life in general, is actually an individual not coming to terms with their own ageing process.*" The tribunal considered that the manager had the claimant, who was 60 years of age, in mind when he made this statement. It was considered reasonable that the claimant perceived the comment as insulting and patronising, leading him to resign. The comments made in the magazine interview were therefore found to be harassment, despite the fact that the comments had not been said or directly addressed to the claimant.

Although in most cases they will, the claimant does not have to be of the same age group towards which harassment is directed in order for the conduct to be unwanted. Further, the alleged harasser does not need to be of a different age group from the claimant. A manager in their early twenties who has quickly risen through the ranks could discriminate against another employee, also in their early twenties, who they consider not up to the job because of their age.

Conduct that is obviously, and by any standard, offensive will be considered inherently unwanted, unless it is expressly invited (***Reed and anor v Stedman*** [1999] IRLR 299, EAT). Where inherently unwanted conduct has occurred, a failure to complain at the time or the fact that the conduct has been continuing for a long period of time without objection will not prevent a claimant from succeeding in their harassment claim.

However, in many cases the conduct in issue will not be obviously offensive. Harassment claims often deal with difficult territory and require tribunals to adjudicate on the fine line between what is "*banter*" or acceptable joking between colleagues and what should be prohibited by law. This is most particularly the case in harassment claims concerning age.

Perhaps because everyone ages, society's approach to comments about age is generally more tolerant than the approach taken to other protected characteristics protected by EqA. This is in general reflected in the tribunal's approach. The tribunal may be less quick to view comments or jokes about age as inherently unwanted when compared to their approach to comments about an individual's race, gender, sexuality or disability.

This view of age will be particularly relevant when practitioners come on to consider whether it is reasonable for the conduct to have had the proscribed effect under s.26 EqA. However, in the most subtle cases, it may also be a factor when the tribunal is considering whether the conduct was unwanted at all.

Where conduct is not inherently unwanted or obviously offensive, the contemporaneous response of the claimant will be relevant evidence that the tribunal may consider. If remarks have been made that some may not consider "*unwanted*", a central consideration for the tribunal will be whether the claimant made it clear that the behaviour was unwelcome. However, the tribunal will of course consider the surrounding context and whether it was possible to express that the conduct was unwelcome. It is open to the tribunal to find that conduct was unwanted even if a claimant chose to remain in employment or chose not to object, either formally or informally (***Munchkins Restaurant Ltd v Karmazyn and Others*** [2010] 1 WLUK 553 (para.23)). As was observed in ***Munchkins Restaurant Ltd***, "*there are many situations in life where people will put up with unwanted or even criminal conduct which violates their personal dignity because they are constrained by social circumstances to do so.*"

The proscribed effect or purpose

There will be harassment if either the *purpose* of the conduct is to create the circumstances described in s.26(1)(b)(i) or (ii) or if that is the *effect* of the conduct, even if it was not intended. A claimant needs only to prove that the conduct had either the effect or the purpose to succeed in their claim of harassment.

Unwanted conduct will have the proscribed effect or purpose if it has the effect or purpose of violating the claimant's dignity or creates an intimidating, hostile, degrading, humiliating, or offensive environment.

The proscribed purpose

In reality, it is often challenging, except in the most egregious and clear-cut cases, to prove the intent of the perpetrator. Many age harassment claims are therefore brought on the basis of the effect of the conduct rather than its purpose.

However, if a harassment claim relies on the alleged purpose of the conduct, the tribunal will have to consider the state of mind of the perpetrator. It will be rare for the perpetrator to clearly state what their intention is, and the tribunal will therefore have to draw inferences as to what their intention might have been. If it has repeatedly been made clear to the perpetrator that their conduct was unwanted or offensive and they persisted regardless, this will be evidence for drawing the inference that there was an intention to create such an environment.

The proscribed effect

If a harassment claim relies on the effect of the conduct, the approach taken by the tribunal is both subjective and objective. Under section 26(4), the tribunal will consider the perception of the claimant, the other circumstances of the case, and whether it is reasonable for the conduct to have the proscribed effect. The focus is on the perception of the claimant, both what it was and what it reasonably might have been. The tribunal, therefore, cannot have regard to conduct of which the claimant was not aware (***Greasley-Adams v Royal Mail Group Ltd*** [2023] EAT 86 (para.20)).

The perception of the claimant and whether they feel the conduct had the proscribed effect is a factual enquiry that will rely heavily on live witness evidence. However, it will not be enough for claimants to assert that they were mildly offended or suffered fleeting upset. For conduct to violate one's dignity, it must be sufficiently serious. Dignity will not necessarily be "*violated by things said or done which are trivial or transitory, particularly if it should have been clear that any offence was unintended*" (***Richmond Pharmacology v Dhaliwal*** [2009] ICR 724, EAT).

When considering what is meant by an intimidating, hostile, degrading, humiliating, or offensive environment, the use of the word "*environment*" in section 26(1)(b)(ii) connotes a state of affairs. There is a difference between a one-off incident and an environment (***General Municipal and Boilermakers Union v Henderson*** [2015] IRLR 451, EAT (para.99)). A single or isolated act can create a state of affairs and may therefore successfully found a harassment claim. However, for it to do so, the isolated incident must reach a degree of seriousness such that it has a more than fleeting impact.

An example is ***Kirk v Citibank NA and Ors*** ET Case No.3200291/18. Mr Kirk had been employed by Citibank for over 26 years and was dismissed in November 2017. The claimant alleged that in a meeting in September 2017, in which he was first informed that his job was at risk, it was said to him: "*you're old and set in your ways.*" The claimant alleged that this single remark amounted to harassment.

The tribunal held that the remark was unwanted conduct, as the comment had upset and angered the claimant, and he had complained about the remark subsequently. Further, the tribunal held that the remark had, both in fact and reasonably, violated the claimant's dignity or created an intimidating, hostile, degrading, humiliating or offensive environment. The claimant had enjoyed a long and successful career with the Respondent, and it was humiliating and insulting to be told he was too old.

This case demonstrates that a single remark is capable of creating the proscribed environment. As is implicit in the decision in ***Kirk***, whether a one-off remark creates an environment relies heavily on the context. The tribunal in ***Kirk*** gave significant weight to the claimant's long and successful career at Citibank when considering what the impact of the remark would reasonably be and whether it was capable of creating the proscribed environment. It is noted that ***Kirk*** was successfully appealed to the EAT. The EAT judgment is considered in greater detail in Chapter 2 of this book. However, the appeal was on the basis that the tribunal had erred in not properly considering the respondent's explanation for the treatment of the claimant, particularly considering the very small age difference between the claimant and his comparator. The consideration of whether a one-off remark could be harassment was not the subject of the appeal.

Different claimants will have very different tolerance levels and responses to unwanted conduct. This is particularly the case with age. Some individuals are sensitive about their age or the topic of aging, whereas others may not see comments or conversations about the subject negatively. However, assertions that conduct has had the proscribed effect will not be accepted by the tribunal without further interrogation. The tribunal may draw inferences from accounts of the claimant's initial reaction to the alleged unwanted conduct.

An example of where a claimant's contemporaneous reaction served as significant evidence of the effect caused by unwanted conduct is ***Bowksill v Select Support Partnerships Ltd*** ET Case No. 2404183/18. In ***Bowskill***, the claimant was a managing director for a company that provided care services to individuals with learning difficulties and other disabilities. In September 2017, it was suggested that the claimant take on a new role in the company. It was further suggested that he was "*too old to take stress and be driving around the country.*" Eleven days later, the claimant sent a letter complaining, among other things, about the ageist and derogatory remarks made against him.

The Tribunal held that the remark had had the effect of violating the claimant's dignity or creating an intimidating, hostile, degrading, humiliating or offensive environment. It was held as significant, when making that finding, that the claimant had complained about the comment in an email within eleven days. This demonstrates that contemporaneous evidence of the claimant's reaction can be a key consideration when considering what the subjective effect of the conduct was on a claimant.

The fact that the claimant participated in the banter or themselves made comments related to their own age will not necessarily mean that they are prevented from contending that the comments made by others had the proscribed effect. It is appreciated that the impact of certain comments will be heightened or changed by who has said them and in what social setting. However, if a claimant has made similar comments themselves, it may suggest that the impact of the comments was less extreme and lead the tribunal to infer that the alleged unwanted conduct did not have the proscribed effect. Even if the tribunal concludes that the conduct did still have the proscribed effect, if the claimant has made similar comments, it may lead to a lower award for injury to feelings when the tribunal come on to consider remedy.

This can be seen in the case of ***Crompton v Eden Private Staff Ltd*** ET Case No. 1404549/19. In ***Crompton***, the claimant, a 57-year-old woman, was in her probationary period as a search consultant when she made some errors in external communications. She was subsequently dismissed for inadequate performance. The tribunal found that the claimant's manager had asked her, on more than one occasion, whether she was suffering from Alzheimer's disease when she forgot things. For example, the claimant's manager had made comments such as, "*is it the Alzheimer's again Mary?*". The tribunal also found that following one of the claimant's mistakes, the claimant herself had sent an email in which she apologised for having a "*senior moment.*"

The tribunal found that the claimant's dismissal was due to performance issues rather than the protected characteristic of age. However, the tribunal did conclude that the comments made by the claimant's manager were unwanted, related to the claimant's age, and created the proscribed state of affairs. The claimant's harassment claim succeeded. However, the claimant's award for injury to feelings was small, falling at only £900 and interest. When determining what injury to feelings award the claimant was entitled to, the tribunal took into account the fact that the claimant had referred to herself as having a '*senior moment.*'

Causation is also important. It is not enough for a claimant to establish that they subjectively experienced the proscribed effect. It must be proved that the proscribed effect was caused by the unwanted conduct.

Was it reasonable for the conduct to have had the effect?

The tribunal will then consider the objective element, namely, whether it is reasonable for conduct to have had the proscribed effect on the claimant. The Court of Appeal has been clear that trivial acts causing minor upsets should not be caught by the concept of harassment (***Land Registry v Grant*** [2011] EWCA Civ 769 (para.47)).

However, whether it is reasonable for remarks or conduct to have had the proscribed effect is a difficult question, particularly in age discrimination cases. As identified in the case of ***XYZ v Birmingham City Council*** ET Case No. 1303436/23, "*in many contexts age-related comments can be friendly and even affectionate and can be meant and taken as harmless and good-humoured.*" As referred to earlier in this chapter, this often sets alleged age harassment claims apart from claims concerning other protected characteristics. Tribunals will often be required, as they were in ***XYZ***, to determine whether comments, which could be considered as affectionate or harmless, have an "*edge*" to them or are "*outside the realms of acceptable workplace banter.*"

In making an objective determination, the tribunal will first have regard to all the circumstances of the case. This was clear in the case of ***Tarbuck v Peninsula Business Services Ltd*** ET Case No. 2404056/14. In ***Tarbuck,*** the claimant alleged that he had been harassed by reason of a comment that he was in the "*pipe and slippers brigade.*" The tribunal acknowledged that it was not surprising that the claimant, who had taken the remark as a suggestion that he worked less hard than other members of staff, was offended. It was therefore clear that the conduct was unwanted. The tribunal also held that the remark could be interpreted as referring to the claimant's age and was therefore related to a protected characteristic.

However, there was a key ingredient missing that led the claimant to fail on his discrimination claim. The tribunal considered it significant that the respondent had been taking steps to retain its experienced members of staff, some of whom were older. Further, there was no evidence that the respondent had a negative perception of the claimant as an older employee. With those circumstances in mind, the tribunal concluded that the remark was "*a trivial, off the cuff comment which cannot objectively be described as creating the effect required for a harassment claim to be made out.*" Regardless of the impact of the remark on the claimant in reality, the tribunal found that it was not reasonable for the conduct to have the serious impact proscribed under s.26.

Tarbuck makes clear that findings on what is objectively reasonable can be shaped by the surrounding circumstances of the workplace, including in some cases broader attitudes towards older or younger employees. While the intent of the perpetrator is not a necessary element, one of the circumstances the tribunal may look to is "*whether it should reasonably have been apparent whether the conduct was, or was not, intended to cause offense*" (***Richmond Pharmacology v Dhaliwal*** [2009] ICR 724, EAT).

This was also underlined in ***Land Registry v Grant*** [2011] EWCA Civ 769 (para.13) in which the Court of Appeal addressed the submission that the intention of the alleged harasser can be relevant only where the purpose of the conduct is in issue. This Court rejected this submission and held that "*everyday experience tells us that a humorous remark between friends may have a very different effect than exactly the same words spoken vindictively by a hostile speaker. It is not importing intent into the concept of effect to say that intent will generally be relevant to assessing effect.*"

The case of ***Palladino v Reed in Partnership*** ET Case No.3303463/2022 similarly demonstrates that comments which the tribunal consider reasonably should not have the proscribed effect will not found successful harassment claims. In ***Palladino*** the claimant alleged that comments made by a younger colleague, that she had "*a lot of experience*", amounted to age-related harassment. The tribunal held that this, amongst other comments made, could not reasonably have the proscribed statutory effect. As a result, the harassment claim was struck out.

A further example of where the claimant failed on the grounds that, while they may have subjectively been upset, the level of upset was not reasonable is ***Munro v Sampson Coward LLP*** ET Case No. 1403495/18.

In ***Munro***, the claimant alleged that she had been harassed by colleagues sending her a card on her 50th birthday and commenting that it had been her 50th birthday. The tribunal did consider that it was relevant context that the claimant was a private person. However, it was also relevant that it was normal practice in the company to mark employees' birthdays by sending a card signed by colleagues. The tribunal therefore found that the card had been intended as an act of kindness and that it could not be regarded as something that would have reasonably had the proscribed effect. The tribunal concluded that the claimant's sensitivity about her age was unusual and extreme.

This case demonstrates that comments made by colleagues that merely report on the objective fact of another colleague's age, even though they have the potential to offend some people who are particularly sensitive about such matters, may not be considered harassment.

Even where words appear to be pejorative, the tribunal will still consider all the surrounding context and circumstances before finding that it was objectively reasonable that the conduct had the proscribed effect. For example, if a manager addressed one of their 50-year-old colleagues as "*old chap*" but also used the same phrase when addressing other younger colleagues, the context may well lead the tribunal to consider that the remark was intended to be friendly and was considered as such by others. The tribunal might therefore conclude that it would not be reasonable for such remarks to have the proscribed effect.

A common example of conduct or behaviour that is often held to have reasonably had the proscribed effect is a suggestion, or a repeated suggestion, that a claimant should retire.

In ***Hutchinson v Asda Stores Ltd*** ET Case No. 1602504/2020, the claimant had been employed by Asda Stores Ltd since September 2000. At the time of her resignation in September 2020, the claimant was 73 years old. From 2017 onwards, the claimant had begun exhibiting signs of dementia. During the lockdown period following the outbreak of Covid-19, the claimant was asked if she wanted to retire. The claimant alleged that she had been asked this regularly. The claimant later resigned following what she alleged to be ongoing harassment and discrimination on the grounds of age and disability. The tribunal found that the option of retirement had been raised with the claimant on more than one occasion and that this was something that would not have been raised with a claimant who was not of retirement age. The tribunal found that this amounted to age-related to harassment. Comments about the claimant retiring had been mentioned on more than one occasion and it was reasonable for the claimant to have formed the impression that she was unwanted or was being pushed out of the business. For more on retirement-related conversations, see Chapter 7 – Retirement.

It is important to remember that when considering whether it was reasonable for conduct to have the proscribed effect on a particular claimant, the tribunal can and will consider circumstances unique to the claimant. For example, previous experiences of harassment or discrimination in general may have reasonably impacted the claimant's tolerance when similar conduct occurs again.

Furthermore, when considering what the reasonable impact of remarks or conduct is, the tribunal should take a cumulative approach. The tribunal should not try and measure the harm caused by each separate remark or incident. Instead, they should look at what the reasonable impact would be of the conduct taken together (***Reed and anor v Stedman*** [1999] IRLR 299).

This was considered most recently by the Court of Appeal in ***Sandhu v Enterprise Rent-A-Car Ltd*** [2025] EWCA Civ 190. This case provides a helpful restatement of the position that a tribunal should not carve up the allegations of harassment and then solely consider them one by one. It is also important to stand back and have regard to the entirety of the conduct which is found to have occurred and what its likely impact would be.

'Related to' age

To succeed on a claim of age-related harassment, the conduct complained of must be related to the protected characteristic of age. Unlike direct discrimination, a comparator does not have to be identified to bring a claim for harassment. However, a comparator may assist in proving that the unwanted conduct was related to age. Conduct can be "*related to*" a claimant's age, even if it was not "*because of*" a claimant's age. This again sets harassment claims apart from those of direct discrimination. The EAT has emphasised that there is no requirement for a mental element equivalent to that required for a claim of direct discrimination (***Carozzi v University of Hertfordshire*** [2024] EAT 169 (para.24)).

The law on what is meant by the phrase "*related to*" was summarised by the Employment Appeal Tribunal in ***Worcestershire Health and Care NHS Trust v Angela Allen*** [2024] EAT 40. The central points were, first, that a finding about the motivation of the alleged harasser is not necessary or the only possible route to the conclusion that an individual's conduct was related to the characteristic in question. Secondly, there must be some feature or features of the factual matrix identified by the tribunal which properly lead it to the conclusion that the conduct in question is related to the protected characteristic in question. Finally, it must be the conduct that is alleged to be harassment that relates to the protected characteristic.

Conduct that is related to age will include conduct that, regardless of the form it takes, is by reason of age. One of the most common examples of conduct that is by reason of age is where employers put pressure on employees to retire. Conduct that is related to age will also include conduct that, regardless of the reason for it, is otherwise related to age because of the form it takes, such as derogatory comments that refer to how many years old an employee is.

Where a direct reference is made to a claimant's age, it will be easy to establish that the behaviour is related to the protected characteristic. An example of this would be where a claimant has been subjected to derogatory remarks that explicitly reference their age. For example, if colleagues joked about a claimant's "*pensioner*" status or routinely described a colleague as "*ancient*" it would be clear that the behaviour was related to the protected characteristic of age.

Direct references to a woman being menopausal will also likely be considered by the tribunal as commentary that is related to age. This was clear in the case of ***A v Bonmarche Ltd*** ET Case No. 4107766/19. The claimant had started her employment with the respondent in 2006. From May 2017 onwards, her manager started to regularly make comments in front of younger members of staff and customers. For example, the claimant was referred to as a "*dinosaur*" when using an iPad to take online orders. Her manager made numerous comments about her being menopausal and linked performance issues to her being menopausal. In May 2018, when the company underwent a restructuring exercise, the claimant's manager asked other members of staff to apply for her job. The claimant also tried to raise issues around the menopause and her symptoms with her manager. However, the claimant's manager refused to speak with her about the matter or adjust the temperature in the shop. The tribunal held that the actions of her manager had amounted to direct discrimination and harassment on the grounds of the claimant being female and of menopausal age.

However, it will not always be so clear whether conduct or certain remarks are related to age. In determining whether the conduct is related to an employee's age, the tribunal will look at all the circumstances, including the context in which the conduct took place (***Warby v Wunda Group plc*** [2012] 1 WLUK 610). In ***Warby***, the employment tribunal highlighted that in some cases the grounds or the reason for the treatment complained of is inherent in the act itself. For example, if an owner of premises puts up a sign saying, "*no blacks admitted*", race is necessarily the ground on which or the reason why a black person is excluded. However, the tribunal highlighted that there will be other cases where the act is not itself discriminatory but is rendered so by a discriminatory motivation. The EAT agreed with that analysis and accepted the position that context is everything. The EAT held that "*it may be a mistake to focus* *upon a remark in isolation. A Tribunal is entitled to take the view, as we see it, that a remark, however unpleasant and unacceptable, is a remark made in a particular context; it is not simply a remark standing on its own.*"

In ***Cubbin v Age UK*** ET Case No. 2210200/2023, the claimant succeeded on one of his claims due to feedback after a job interview which contained the phrase: "*the standard of his layout and typographical skills are not reflective of 40 years' experience*". The tribunal found that the respondent imposed a higher standard upon the claimant than the "*must have*" for the role and this would not have been said of a candidate with 5 years' experience. It therefore found that Mr Cubbin had been subject to harassment as the comment was "*plainly related to his age*". It is a reminder that a critical comment implying that someone should know better due to their experience, may be found to be related to age.

An alleged harasser does not need to have used ageist language or have engaged in behaviour that is overtly age specific before a harassment claim can be made out under s.26 EqA. However, where the link between the conduct and the protected characteristic is less obvious, tribunals may need to go further and analyse the context, the precise words used and consider the mental processes of the alleged harasser to determine whether the conduct is related to age.

In ***Osborne and another v Gondhia and others t/a Rutaba Partnership*** ET Case No. 3401426/14 and 3401427/14, the tribunal held that the heavy criticism that the claimants had been subjected to was related to their age, despite no direct reference to their age. The first claimant was 21 at the time of her dismissal, and the second claimant was 18. They contended that they were subject to unjustified criticism in front of customers because they were both young and female. The tribunal held that the respondents would not have treated the claimants in the same way if they were either a man or more mature. This demonstrates that to establish that conduct is related to age, direct or explicit reference to age may not be necessary. In ***Osborne,*** the tribunal held that the surrounding context and the way that other employees were treated was sufficient to establish that the conduct was related to the claimants' age.

The EAT have however made clear that the mere fact that conduct concerns or relates to a complaint of age discrimination will not be sufficient to mean that unwanted conduct is necessarily related to age. In ***Worcestershire Health and Care NHS Trust v Angela Allen*** [2024] EAT 40, the ET had found that the predetermination of the claimant's grievance, which in part concerned age discrimination, constituted age-related harassment. The only connection that the ET had found between the claimant's age and the grievance process was that the grievance included an allegation of age discrimination. However, there was nothing that connected the prejudgment of the grievance outcome with the claimant's age. The EAT highlighted that no ageist language was used by the grievance panel that could have led to the conclusion that the outcome they reached was related to age. For the ET to have determined that the outcome of the grievance was related to age, they would therefore have had to consider the mental process of the grievance panel. The ET had not done so and had seemingly relied only on the fact that the grievance referred to age discrimination. The harassment claim therefore should not have succeeded.

Harassment by association or perception

The use of the words "*related to*" in section 26 EqA makes clear that the EqA will cover unwanted conduct that is motivated by a claimant's association with individuals with a protected characteristic or because of a false perception that an employee has a protected characteristic, even if they do not.

If a claimant has been subjected to unwanted conduct that had the proscribed effect because of a false perception that they have a certain protected characteristic, they will be able to bring a claim for harassment (***English v Thomas Sanderson Ltd*** [2008] EWCA Civ 1421). It is therefore possible for employees who look either younger or older than they are to bring claims for harassment if they are subjected to unwanted conduct because of their perceived age.

Protection from third-party harassment

Previously, the EqA protected employees from third-party harassment that they experienced from contractors or customers. However, this was repealed from 1 October 2013 by the Enterprise Regulatory Reform Act 2013 and will not be considered any further in this chapter. There is no explicit liability on an employer for failing to prevent third-party harassment, as was emphasised by the EAT in ***Bessong v Pennine Care NHS Foundation Trust*** [2020] IRLR 4. The Worker Protection (Amendment of Equality Act 2010) Act 2023, which came into effect from 26 October 2024, provides a limited "*preventative duty*" which applies solely to sexual harassment and is therefore not relevant to a consideration of harassment related to age.

However, the failure of an employer to protect an employee from a third party could still be considered harassment if it can be established that that failure was unwanted conduct, that had the proscribed effect, and that the failure was related to the protected characteristic of age.

It is also noted that in October 2024, the Labour Government introduced the Employment Rights Bill to Parliament. This Bill would impose a duty to take all reasonable steps to prevent harassment of employees at work, including by third parties. This would not be limited solely to sexual harassment but would apply to harassment of any kind, including harassment related to age. Explicit liability for third-party harassment may therefore return in the near future.

The most recent update at the time of writing has been the 'implementation roadmap' for the Employment Rights Bill, published on 1 July 2025. Based on the roadmap, employer liability for third-party harassment will likely come into force in October 2026. Practitioners are therefore advised to follow the progress of the Employment Rights Bill and its implementation closely.

CHAPTER SIX

VICTIMISATION

- *Has a protected act been done?*
- *Has the claimant been subject to a detriment?*
- *Was the claimant subjected to the detriment because of the protected act?*

Section 27 Equality Act ("EqA") 2010 protects claimants from victimisation. Victimisation refers to a situation where a person (A) subjects another person (B) to a detriment because B does a protected act or A believes that B has done, or may do, a protected act. A similar legal concept is called '*retaliation*' in the United States, which perhaps describes more clearly exactly what it is. This chapter focuses solely on bringing victimisation claims where B does a protected act that concerns, or allegedly concerns, the protected characteristic of age.

It is important to note that, as was made clear in the case of ***Rowstock Ltd and Anor v Jessemy*** [2014] EWCA Civ 185, s.27 can cover situations where a former employee is subject to a detriment by a former employer because they have performed a protected act. To bring a claim for post-termination victimisation, the claimant must meet the normal requirements of section 108(1) Equality Act 2010 ('EqA'). Namely, the conduct complained of, if it had occurred during employment, must have contravened the EqA and the conduct must have arisen out of or be closely connected to the past employment relationship.

Protected Act

There are five categories of behaviour that can amount to a protected act.

Four of these are set out under section 27(2) EqA. These are:

(a) Bringing proceedings under this Act;

(b) Giving evidence or information in connection with proceedings under the Act;

(c) Doing any other thing for the purposes of or in connection with this Act;

(d) Making an allegation (whether or not express) that A or another person has contravened this Act.

The fifth category is discussed below under 'pay disclosure protected acts'.

Section 27 sets out that the first question is whether a claimant has performed one of the protected acts, or if the discriminator believes that the claimant has done or may do a protected act.

However, the protected act does not actually have to have been performed, or believed to be performed, by the claimant themselves. A claimant need only establish that a protected act has been done and that they were subsequently subjected to a detriment because of it. Section 27 has been read this way to make it consistent with the Equal Treatment Directive. As a result, it is possible to bring a claim for associative victimisation. This was made clear in ***Mr G Thompson v London Central Bus Co*** [2016] IRLR 9 EAT. In ***Thompson***, the claimant held that he had been disciplined because he was associated in the mind of his employer with others who had raised complaints about racism and therefore done protected acts. The central question is whether the treatment of the claimant was by reason of his association with another who made protected acts.

What does it mean to 'bring proceedings under the Act'? (Section 27(2)(a))

Bringing proceedings under the Equality Act is one of the clearest ways to perform a protected act. In reality, victimisation claims that rely on an employee bringing proceedings usually concern situations where employees suffer retribution because of earlier proceedings that they have brought. However, this section would also apply to concurrent EqA proceedings.

The most obvious example of bringing proceedings under the Act will be issuing proceedings in the Employment Tribunal against one's employer for a breach of the EqA. However, it is important to remember that s.27(2)(a) covers any and all proceedings brought under the EqA. The proceedings do not need to have been brought against the employer who is later accused of victimisation. Section 27(2)(a) will also include proceedings brought against a previous employer or even a service provider. If a claimant brought age discrimination proceedings in the county court against a university where they took night classes and was subsequently subjected to a detriment by their line manager at work who labelled them a troublemaker, their claim against the university would amount to a protected act under s.27(2)(a). Similarly, if word got around that an employee had brought age discrimination proceedings against a previous employer, those earlier proceedings would amount to a protected act.

A victimisation claim is not dependent on the success of the proceedings that were brought as part of the protected act. A tribunal will not dismiss a victimisation claim just because another court or tribunal have rejected the underlying claims of discrimination which formed the protected act.

What does it mean to 'give evidence or information in connection with proceedings under this Act'? (Section 27(2)(b))

The second example of conduct that amounts to a protected act is giving evidence or information in connection with proceedings under the EqA.

This subsection is most often relied on in situations where an employee has given evidence for a colleague in employment tribunal proceedings and alleges that they later suffered reprisals from their employer. Evidence only needs to be given 'in connection' with proceedings. Giving evidence in preparation for a hearing will also amount to a protected act as well as giving evidence in the hearing itself. For example, if employee A issues an employment tribunal claim for direct age discrimination and asks their colleague, employee B, to provide a witness statement, the act of providing the witness statement will constitute a protected act, even if the matter has not yet been heard.

However, for evidence to be given 'in connection' with proceedings, proceedings must exist. This means that proceedings need to have been instigated. If colleagues were asked to provide statements or evidence before the proceedings had been started, it would not, under subsection 27(2)(b), be considered a protected act. However, providing a statement or evidence at an earlier stage may be seen as doing some 'other thing' in connection with the Act under s.27(2)(c). It may therefore still be possible to establish that there was a protected act, albeit under a different section.

The EqA and section 27 will not protect any employee who gives evidence or information which they know to be false. However, that does not mean that all the information or evidence provided must be true. If the evidence was given in good faith, it will be a protected act, even if it later proved to be inaccurate. The requirement that alleged protected acts be done in good faith is considered in further detail later in this chapter.

What does it mean to 'do any other thing for the purpose of or in connection with this Act' (Section 27(2)(c))

The third type of conduct that will be considered a protected act is doing any other thing for the purpose of or in connection with the EqA. This section is intentionally broad. This provision can be seen as a catch-all to ensure protection for other conduct or complaints that might fall through the gaps of the other provisions.

What can be considered 'any other thing' for the purpose of or in connection with the EqA is not wholly clear from the wording of the EqA. In ***Bayfield and Anor v Wundermand Thompson (UK) Ltd and ors*** ET Case No.2200540/2019, the question of what was meant by 'in connection' was considered by the tribunal.

The claimants in ***Bayfield*** were employed by the first respondent, the UK arm of a global advertising agency. The claimants brought claims of sex, age, sexual orientation, and race discrimination, unfair and automatically unfair dismissal, and victimisation. In ***Bayfield***, both the claimants had complained about a presentation given by two of the first respondent's employees at an industry conference. It was alleged that this complaint was a protected act. The presentation given was titled "*Crisis: The Mother of All Change*". The presentation addressed recent gender pay gap figures that had been published, which showed that the mean gender pay gap at the first respondent was 38.8% and the median gender pay gap was 44.7%. One of the slides was titled "*White, British, Privileged, Straight, Men Creating Traditional Above the Line Advertising.*" Elements of this presentation were picked up by the press and articles were published with headlines such as "*Inside JWTs plan to address its 'terrible' gender pay gap & 'boys' club' reputation.*" On hearing about this presentation, the claimants sent emails stating that they had "*found out recently JWT did a talk off site where it vowed to obliterate white middle class straight people from its creative department. There are a lot of very worried people down here.*" The claimants alleged that by sending such emails they were doing something in connection with the EqA.

The tribunal noted that there was no explicit reference to age in the emails or to the EqA. Further, some of the characteristics referred to in the email, such as '*privileged*' and '*middle-class*', are not protected characteristics. The tribunal did conclude however that the claimants were genuinely worried that male, straight, privileged, white creatives who created traditional advertising might be dismissed because of the presentation. The tribunal found that there is a wide interpretation given to the meaning of '*doing any other thing in connection with the Act*' and that the claimants' emails would fall into that category. The claimants were saying they believed their jobs were at risk on grounds which included their sex, sexual orientation and race, and therefore they were doing something in connection with the EqA.

What does it mean to 'make an allegation (whether or not express) that a person has contravened this Act'? (section 27(2)(d))

The final type of conduct referred to in s.27 that will be judged as a protected act are allegations that another person has contravened the EqA. The allegation in question does not have to have been made about the alleged victimiser, nor does the EqA specify to whom the allegations must have been made.

The focus of the tribunal will be to consider the substance and the character of what was said, not whether allegations explicitly refer to the EqA. If the allegation does not need to refer explicitly to the EqA, what does the allegation have to contain for it to be considered a protected act under section 27(2)(d)?

The answer is that the claimant must have asserted facts that are capable of amounting to an actionable breach of the EqA. Case law suggests that this will usually require more than a mere assertion that an employer's behaviour might be unlawful or discriminatory. That assertion will usually need to be supported by further explanation or facts that suggest a breach of the EqA. For example, complaining that an employer's new pension policy may be unlawful is, of itself, unlikely to be considered a protected act. However, if a claimant complained that an employer's new pension policy might be unlawful because it put new employees, who were by definition younger, at a disadvantage, they may well be able to establish that they had performed a protected act within the scope of s.27(2)(d).

There may also be cases where a claimant asserts that they have experienced discrimination but fails to specify which protected characteristic the allegation relates to. This was considered in ***Durrani v London Borough of Ealing*** UKEAT/0454/2012. The EAT stated that they would "*accept that it is not necessary that the complaint referred to race using that very word. But there must be something sufficient about the complaint to show that it is a complaint to which at least potentially the Act applies.*"

When considering whether there has been an allegation that a person has contravened the EqA where there has been no explicit reference to the EqA, the tribunal will look at the nature of the complaint in the round. For example, if an 65 year-old employee made a complaint that they had been bullied but in that same complaint asserted that their line manager had also bullied other colleagues in their team who were 26 and 35, it is unlikely that, taking the nature of the complaint as a whole, the tribunal will consider that it amounts to an allegation under s.27(2)(d). This was the position of the EAT in ***Mr H S Fullah v Medical Research Council and anor*** EAT 0586/12 (para.26) which concerned claims of race discrimination. In ***Fullah,*** the EAT found that the tribunal had been right to find there was no protected act because the claimant was "*complaining with his fellow employees, who were not black and did not make claims of race discrimination*" about the same individual.

The tribunal will always look at the surrounding context. When considering whether a qualifying allegation is implied the tribunal can look beyond the claimant's spoken words or at other comments they have made (***Page v Lord Chancellor and Anor*** [2021] ICR 912 CA (para.51)). Looking beyond the words used by a claimant will be particularly important when a claimant has made a written complaint that is incredibly vague. For example, if a claimant has submitted a complaint that their employer's behaviour "*may be discriminatory*" without further supporting context or evidence, a Tribunal is unlikely to find that such a vague comment amounts to a protected act (***Mrs L Chalmers v Airpoint Ltd & Others*** [2020] 12 WLUK 545 (paras.16-17).

However, the surrounding context might be able to provide necessary clarity as to what the alleged breach of the EqA is. An example of this would be if an employee had previously asked their manager about how the company bonus policy worked and whether they thought the policy might be unfair for younger staff members. If that employee were then to email their line manager and ask for a meeting "*to discuss their earlier concerns, particularly that the company bonus policy may be discriminatory*", a tribunal would be more likely to conclude, with reference to the surrounding context, that the claimant had done a protected act.

What happens when a claimant has acted in "bad faith"

Allegations made, evidence provided, or proceedings brought do not have to succeed or be proved to be true to amount to a protected act. However, s.27(3) EqA is clear that "*giving false evidence or information or making a false allegation is not a protected act if the evidence or information is given, or the allegation is made, in bad faith.*"

When considering what is meant by the phrase "*bad faith*" in the context of s.27(3) EqA 2010, the central question is whether the claimant acted honestly in giving the evidence or information or in making the allegation. Often, respondents will seek to rely on s.27(3) where a claimant has intentionally performed or manufactured a protected act as set out under s.27 with a view to later bringing a victimisation claim. However, it was made clear in ***Saad v Southampton University Hospitals NHS Trust*** [2019] ICR 311 (para.52) that, while motivation may be part of the relevant context, the primary focus will be on the employee's honesty. If a tribunal finds that a claimant subjectively believed their allegation to be true at the time, then the claimant will have acted in good faith.

Pay disclosure protected acts

As set out at the start of this chapter, there are five types of behaviour that can amount to a protected act. Four of those are set out in s.27 EqA. The fifth category of behaviour that can amount to a protected act is set out under s.77 EqA and concerns situations where employees are seeking to share information about pay disparities that may be correlated with protected characteristics.

A relevant pay disclosure will be a protected act within the meaning of the Equality Act. A disclosure will be considered a 'relevant pay disclosure' where it is made for the purpose of enabling the person who makes it, or the person to whom it is made, to find out whether or to what extent there is, in relation to the work in question, a connection between pay and having (or not having) a particular protected characteristic.

As is made clear in s.77(4)(b), making or seeking to make a relevant pay disclosure will certainly be a protected act. However, seeking or receiving information from a pay disclosure is also a protected act under s.77(4)(a) and (c) EqA. Therefore, perhaps surprisingly, if an employee is told that they are making less than an older colleague doing the same role, they may well, under s.77(4)(c) have done a protected act, despite the fact that they have only been the recipient of information.

Whether or not a pay disclosure under s.77(4) is subject to the requirement of good faith under s.27(3), s.77(3) appears to require good faith in any event, because it specifies that the purpose of the pay disclosure must be to enable the recipient to find out *'whether or to what extent'* there is a connection between pay and a protected characteristic. It does not require that there is in fact a connection, and the disclosure would be a protected act even if the discloser was mistaken as to whether there was a connection, as long as the purpose of the discloser was to enable the recipient to find out about such a connection. The wording of the statute implies that the person communicating must have a genuine desire to communicate a pay disparity. This would appear to exclude anyone acting in bad faith.

Detriment

The concept of a "detriment" has been given a broad interpretation by the tribunal. If a reasonable worker would or might take the view that the treatment was in all the circumstances to his or her disadvantage, then they will have been subjected to a detriment (***Shamoon v Chief Constable of the Royal Ulster Constabulary*** [2003] ICR 337, HL).

It is important to note that, despite reference to the 'reasonable worker', this is not an entirely objective test. The test has both subjective and objective elements. It is not enough for a claimant to simply assert that they suffered mental distress to establish that there was a detriment. Equally, it is not for the tribunal objectively to decide what they think amounts to a disadvantage in their view. The tribunal will consider the position from the claimant's perspective and then consider whether the claimant's sense of grievance is justified with regard to all the circumstances of the case. Where a tribunal finds that a reasonable worker could take the view that, in all the circumstances, the conduct was to the worker's detriment, then, even if the tribunal itself does not consider that the conduct was detrimental, the test will be satisfied (***Warburton v Chief Constable of Northamptonshire Police*** [2022] EAT 42 (para.51)).

When considering whether treatment was in all the circumstances to the claimant's disadvantage, it is not appropriate to "*pursue the treatment and its consequences down to an end result in order to try and demonstrate that the complainant is, in the end better off, or at least no worse off, than he would have been if he had not been treated differently. I think it suffices if the complainant can reasonably say that he would have preferred not to have been treated differently*" (***Chief Constable of West Yorkshire Police v Khan*** [2001] UKHL 48 (para.76)).

Case law is clear that omissions to act, most commonly the refusal to provide a reference, can be a detriment. However, if the detriment complained of is an omission, care will have to be taken to identify the date of the omission and ensure that the claim is in time (see Chapter 10, under 'Time limits/extensions of time').

Conduct that is considered a detriment under section 27 EqA cannot be conduct that amounts to harassment under section 26 EqA, as is set out under section 212(1) EqA. This does not mean that practitioners cannot bring claims for both harassment and victimisation arising from the same facts, however they must be pleaded in the alternative. It may therefore be helpful to consider strategically whether there is an advantage to bringing a claim for both harassment and victimisation. Arguing victimisation and harassment in the alternative may, in some cases, undermine arguments that the claimant was subjected to particular treatment for a particular reason.

'Because of' the protected act

If a claimant can establish that they have suffered a detriment, they must then prove that they suffered this detriment because of the protected act. This is often the most challenging element when bringing a victimisation claim. If the claimant experienced a detriment because of their own misconduct or because of an unrelated or separable breakdown of a personal relationship, then the claim of victimisation cannot succeed.

The phrase 'because of' holds the same meaning as in a claim for direct discrimination, which is discussed in further detail in Chapter 2 on Direct Age Discrimination. The central question will be what, either consciously or subconsciously, motivated the employer to subject the claimant to the detriment. Importantly, the test to be applied is not one of 'but for' causation (***Chief Constable of West Yorkshire Police v Khan*** [2001] ICR 1065, HL).

Instead, the focus of the tribunal must be on identifying the real reason for the treatment complained of. This will require consideration of the victimiser's state of mind. The tribunal need not distinguish between conscious and subconscious motivation when determining whether a complainant has been victimised. If the victimiser subconsciously allowed the protected act to influence their treatment of the claimant, then the detriment will be 'because of' the protected act (***Nagarajan v London Regional Transport*** [1999] ICR 877 HL). An employer will not be able to escape liability because they can show that they did not intend to discriminate against a claimant.

Of course, it follows from this that for the detriment to be 'because of' a claimant's protected act, the person who inflicted the detriment must know about the protected act. Without that knowledge, the claim of victimisation cannot succeed (***Scott v London Borough of Hillingdon***

[2001] EWCA Civ 2005 CA (para.9)). Guidance in ***Chief Constable of Cumbria v McGlennon*** [2002] ICR 1156, makes it clear that whether the victimiser had knowledge of the claimant's protected act is something the tribunal should consider and address in their decision.

It has been made clear that the tribunal cannot attribute a principal's knowledge of a protected act to an agent. There is case law in the sphere of whistleblowing that has considered the question of whether the knowledge and motivation of a principal can be imparted to an unknowing agent. These are usually situations where a principal becomes aware of a claimant's protected disclosure and, in retribution, passes on tainted or inaccurate information to an agent who goes on to subject the claimant to a detriment based on a genuine belief in that tainted information. It will be interesting to see if this case law can be transposed to victimisation cases. However, the current position under the EqA is that the focus must be on the motivation of the actual decision maker who has subjected the claimant to a detriment, as was set out by the Court of Appeal in ***Reynolds v CLIFS (UK) Ltd and ors*** [2015] EWCA Civ 439 (para.46). The Court of Appeal held that the acts of those who have provided 'tainted information' to a decision maker for unlawful reasons would have to be considered separately from the actions of the innocent decision maker. However, it may be that a separate victimisation claim can be brought concerning the actions of the principal. In passing on tainted information about the claimant, the principal will likely have subjected the claimant to a detriment.

A failure to investigate a complaint of discrimination will rarely constitute victimisation in and of itself under section 27. The reason for this is that it will often be hard to establish that there was a link between the fact of the employee raising a complaint or grievance and the subsequent failure to investigate it (***A v Chief Constable of West Midlands Police*** EAT 0313/14 (para.22)).

However, if an employer puts forward an inadequate explanation or no explanation at all for their failure to investigate a grievance, the tribunal may draw the inference that the real reason for the failure was the claimant's protected act. Even if the real reason for a failure to investigate is something that some respondents might be reluctant to draw attention to, such as incompetence, it is in a respondent's interests to put forward a positive explanation of why a complaint has not been dealt with in a timely manner.

An example of the tribunal drawing inferences from an inadequate explanation for certain behaviour is ***Benassi v Maximus UK Services limited*** ET Case No. 2304842/2022. This case concerned an 18-year-old woman who worked as an employment adviser. She alleged that having raised a grievance, she suffered three detriments, namely, the failure to investigate her allegation of age discrimination, the decision to demote her to the role of receptionist, and finally the decision to dismiss her. The tribunal held that the grievance, which stated that "*continuous targeting stems from my age as I do not believe she would do this to me had I been older*" was a protected act. The tribunal considered that while there had been tensions before the claimant's grievance was raised, there did appear to have been an increase in scrutiny of the claimant and her work following the grievance being made. The tribunal also found it significant that HR, who were contacted, were reluctant to sanction the dismissal. The evidence suggested that the dismissal was essentially forced through against HR advice. The decision to dismiss in that context called out for an explanation. Furthermore, 95% of employees at the respondent company passed their probation without any difficulties. The dismissal in this situation was therefore abnormal. The tribunal concluded that the burden of proof shifted and that it was for the respondent to justify why the dismissal was not because of the protected act. The tribunal found that, while there had been some performance issues, there was no satisfactory explanation as to why the claimant had been dismissed after three months. They therefore drew the inference that the dismissal was because of the protected act, and the claim of victimisation was upheld. This case is instructive as an example of inferences that tribunals may draw when a respondent provides no positive explanation for certain conduct, such as dismissal or a failure to investigate a grievance (see further in Chapter 8 Proving age discrimination).

However, when considering whether a detriment was suffered because of a protected act, it is important to keep in mind that the protected act need not be the only reason for the treatment, or even the main reason. It is enough to show that the discriminatory reason was given "sufficient weight" (***O'Donoghue v Redcar and Cleveland Borough Council*** [2001] EWCA Civ 701). As was set out by Lord Nicholls in the case of ***Nagarajan v London Regional Transport*** [1999] IRLR 572, decisions are frequently reached for more than one reason, but if "*protected acts had a significant influence on the outcome, discrimination is made out.*" It will therefore not be destructive to a claimant's claim if multiple causes were at play. Equally, from the respondent's perspective, highlighting that there was another reason for applying a detriment to a claimant that was not the protected act will not always serve as a complete defence.

There are sometimes cases where, in successfully proving that there has been a long and ongoing campaign of harassment or direct discrimination, it will be difficult to prove that any detriment was 'because of' a protected act. This is what happened in the case of ***Dooley v Williams; WM Functions Limited; Woolston Manor Golf Club Limited*** ET Case No. 3200819/2018. The claimant had been working at Woolston Golf Club since 10 April 2007 and was 49 years old when her employment started. The claimant was promoted to the role of Sales Manager in January 2017. An associate director, Mr Lee Williams, had been making comments about the claimant's age since January 2017. For example, the claimant was told, "*computers are for young people – not you.*" The claimant was also told that she was "*too old for this*" and that she was "*past it*". In August 2017, the claimant made a complaint about Mr Williams and a staff meeting was held in response. In January 2018, the claimant's employment was terminated with immediate effect after she refused a different position offered to her.

The claimant brought allegations of direct age discrimination, age-related harassment and victimisation. The tribunal found that the complaints submitted by the claimant in August 2017 were a protected act. The tribunal held that the claimant had been harassed and directly discriminated against because of her age, however, the claimant had been harassed by Mr Williams on the grounds of age for a long period of time before she lodged the complaint and there was no clear evidence that the pattern of harassment changed after the complaint was made. Furthermore, there was a gap of five months between the grievance being raised and the claimant's dismissal. As a result, the claimant's victimisation claim failed.

There is also a line of case law that demonstrates that it is possible to argue that the detrimental treatment was not because of the protected act itself but because of some specific feature of the complaint or the way it was made. If a detriment is inflicted because of the manner in which the protected act was carried out, for example if an employee "*makes, in good faith, a complaint of discrimination but couches it in terms of violent racial abuse of the manager responsible*" it would not be victimisation to take action against that employee (***Martin v Devonshires Solicitors*** [2011] ICR 352 EAT (para.22)). This position was affirmed by the Court of Appeal in ***Page v NHS Trust Development Authority*** [2021] EWCA Civ 254.

There is no time limit or limitation period that applies to the period of time between the protected act being done and the detriment being suffered. However, the more time that elapses after the claimant has done the protected act, the harder it will become to show that the detriment was applied because of the protected act.

An example of this would be if a claimant brought an age discrimination claim over her employer's decision to reduce her hours while remaining in employment. If the claimant was subsequently accused of gross misconduct and dismissed three weeks later, a tribunal would be likely to take into account the timing of the allegations of misconduct. That would be an important factor when considering whether the claimant's employment tribunal claim had a significant influence on the decision to dismiss the claimant.

CHAPTER SEVEN

RETIREMENT

- *Employers can implement compulsory retirement ages but they must be justified.*

- *Tried and tested legitimate aims are intergenerational fairness, workplace planning and dignity for older employees.*

- *Both the principle of mandatory retirement and the specific age for retirement must be proportionate.*

- *Care needs to be taken with conversations about retirement with regard to pressure and the timing.*

Introduction

Prior to 2011, it did not constitute age discrimination to dismiss an employee over the age of 65 if the reason for dismissal was retirement (Sch 9 Equality Act 2010, s8). Equally, it did not constitute age discrimination to turn down an application for employment on the basis that the applicant was over 65 or the normal retirement age of the employer. 65 was the national default retirement age.

Moreover, regarding the law of unfair dismissal, retirement was one of the potentially fair reasons for dismissal under the Employment Rights Act 1996, along with capability, conduct, redundancy and 'some other substantial reason'. As long as the employer followed a set procedure of notification and consideration of any alternative option (set out in Schedule 6, Employment Equality (Age) Regulations 2006), the dismissal would unlikely be either unfair or discriminatory.

Since the Employment Equality (Repeal of Retirement Age Provisions) Regulations 2011 came into force in April 2011, many of the above provisions have been repealed. This means that any dismissal for retirement must be justified in the same way as any other provision, criterion or practice that creates a particular disadvantage in relation to age. There is no longer a default retirement age. Similarly, retirement is no longer a potentially fair reason for dismissal and any dismissal for retirement would have to come under the umbrella of 'some other substantial reason' and will inevitably involve a consideration of whether the retirement age was justified.

In short, it is now harder to ask employees to retire and employees over 65 are better protected under equality legislation than they have been historically.

Can employers still retire employees?

Yes – this can still be done. However, more consideration is needed than before.

Many employers have now done away with a compulsory retirement age. Some organisations maintain mandatory retirement – both Oxford and Cambridge University currently set that age at 69 and have policies on extensions. The judiciary also has a mandatory retirement age of 75. Fire services may also have normal retirement ages.

The key point is to be able to justify why a compulsory retirement age is needed. ***R (on the application of Age (UK) v Secretary of State for Business, Innovation and Skills*** [2009] IRLR 1017 is the case that arguably led to the change in law in 2011. Age UK challenged the Default Retirement Age of 65. The High Court accepted that the government had proven to the appropriate standard that the decision to implement a default retirement age was both proportionate and legitimate due to social policy concerns in protecting the integrity of the labour market and maintaining confidence in it. However, *per curiam,* Blake J questioned whether the choice of 65 as the age was proportionate.

Given that it is almost always clear that retiring individuals will constitute less favourable treatment because of age, the focus of the case law is on justification – i.e. legitimate aims and whether they are achieved by proportionate means.

Legitimate aims

The importance of formulating legitimate aims

In ***Seldon v Clarkson Wright and Jakes*** [2012] UKSC 16, the Supreme Court tackled the question of a mandatory contractual retirement age for partners in a law firm. It also gives useful illustrations of different legitimate aims and what might and might not succeed in an argument of justification.

Mr Seldon was made to retire on 31 December 2006. It is noteworthy that, as a partner, he was not an employee. At the time, the default retirement age was still in force for employees. However, this did not apply to him and so the law firm had to justify the mandatory retirement age in the same way they would have to do for any employee post 2011.

As Mr Seldon neared the age of 65, which was the firm's mandatory retirement age for partners, he realised he needed to work for another three years for personal financial reasons. He therefore proposed to the other partners that he stay on. They refused on the basis that there was no business case to do so. He was dismissed by reason of retirement.

In justifying the compulsory retirement age, the respondent sought to rely on six legitimate aims. The tribunal at first instance accepted the following three as genuine aims which can be summarised respectively as staff retention, workforce planning and dignity:

- Ensuring that associates are given the opportunity of partnership after a reasonable period as an associate, thereby ensuring that associates do not leave the firm;

- Facilitating the planning of the partnership and workforce across individual departments by having a realistic long-term expectation as to when vacancies will arise;

- Limiting the need to expel partners by way of performance management, thus contributing to a congenial and supportive culture in the Respondent firm.

With regard to proportionality, the ET accepted that the first two aims could only be implemented through a compulsory retirement age – there was no other way of doing it. As for the dignity aim, it found that introducing performance management of older partners would be uncertain and demeaning. On remittal, the ET and EAT also found that the specific age of 65 was justified (***Seldon v Clarkson Wright and Jakes*** *(No.2)* [2014] ICR 1275).

The Supreme Court agreed with the ET that all three aims were legitimate (para 67). It explained that the first two aims are directly related to the established social policy aim of intergenerational fairness – i.e. sharing out professional employment opportunities between generations (re the European case of ***Fuchs and another v Land Hessen,*** Joined Cases C-159/10 and C-160/10, [2011] 3 CMLR 1299). The third aim – limiting the need to subject partners nearing the end of the career to performance management – had also been established in ***Fuchs*** as well as in ***Rosenbladt v Oellerking* GmbH,** Case C-45/09, [2011] CMLR 1011.

Lady Hale noted that (1) intergenerational fairness and (2) dignity were the two main categories of legitimate aim in the case law. She commented however (para 57) that the aim of dignity is the far more controversial of the two as it effectively relies on the stereotype that older people may become less capable – which may be true of some but not others. Therefore, we note that whilst the legitimate aim of dignity is firmly established as potentially legitimate, it would be sensible to rely on other aims alongside it.

It is of interest to note that the original tribunal did not accept that three other aims were genuine aims of the firm. Whilst it cannot be said these aims would not be accepted in other contexts, there is far less basis in case law for these. They can be summarised as career progression, financial planning and maintaining a partnership model:

- Ensuring that there is a turnover of partners such that any partner can expect to become Senior Partner in due course;
- Enabling and encouraging employees and partners to make adequate financial provision for retirement;
- Protecting the partnership model of the Respondent. If equity partners could not be forced to retire at 65, but employees (including salaried partners) could be, it would be preferable to keep lawyers at the Respondent as employees or salaried partners rather than equity partners.

General examples of legitimate aims relating to age

The Supreme Court also reviewed European case law (para 50) and drew the following examples of aims which had been recognised as legitimate in age discrimination claims and may therefore be useful for employers thinking about what their legitimate aims are:

- Promoting access to employment for younger people;
- The efficient planning of the departure and recruitment of staff;
- Sharing out employment opportunities fairly between the generations;
- Ensuring a mix of generations of staff so as to promote the exchange of experience and new ideas;
- Rewarding experience;

- Cushioning the blow for long serving employees who may find it hard to find new employment if dismissed;
- Facilitating the participation of older workers in the workforce;
- Avoiding the need to dismiss employees on the ground that they are no longer capable of doing the job which may be humiliating for the employee concerned;
- Avoiding disputes about the employee's fitness for work over a certain age.

The aim must be genuine in the circumstances of the case

A word of warning – Lady Hale noted (para 59) that just because a stated aim is capable of being a legitimate aim does not mean it is actually the aim being pursued. For example, with regard to intergenerational fairness, if there is not in reality an issue with recruiting young people and/or the issue is more a failure to retain experienced staff, then a stated aim of providing opportunities to young people might not be legitimate. Equally if the organisation has a good performance management system in place that works well, it may not be a legitimate aim to want to avoid using it (para 61). Taking this further, even if the legitimate aim is established, there may be an issue with establishing proportionality if, for example, a company is not in fact struggling to recruit young people as the retirement age will not be reasonably necessary to achieve the aim.

Furthermore, the aim does not need to have been thought of at the time when the measure was first adopted, it can be rationalised after the event, as long as it is genuine.

The consequence of both the above points is that employers need to give good witness evidence, backed up by documentary evidence if possible, on what its genuine legitimate aims were and why they were necessary. Statistical evidence – for example on difficulties in recruiting or retaining staff – can also be very valuable (see Chapter 3 on indirect age discrimination and Chapter 8 on proving age discrimination for more on statistics).

Is it enough to justify the general policy or does each particular instance of retirement need to be justified?

A further point considered by the Supreme Court in ***Seldon*** was whether a respondent would need only to justify the retirement clause generally or also to justify it in relation to the particular circumstances of the individual bringing a claim. For example, if a legitimate aim is intergenerational fairness then does an employer need to show that an associate would be promoted as a result of the claimant being retired? The Court of Appeal did not find this was necessary. The Supreme Court agreed essentially on the basis that the whole point of justifying a general policy is that it means that it should be justified whenever it is applied (para 65). However, Lady Hale noted that there may be factors specific to the individual which would be relevant to the argument of justification. She noted that in Mr Seldon's case, when considering whether his forced retirement was proportionate, it must be relevant that he was one of the partners that negotiated the rule. It would also be relevant if he had previously had the benefit of a partner retiring to make way for him earlier in his career. Both of those facts, she implied, would go in favour of the decision being proportionate. Equally it may be relevant if an employee is not told of the policy of a mandatory retirement age until a year before retirement, such that she is not given the opportunity to plan financially.

We would recommend therefore that parties provide evidence on the particular circumstances of the individual if they can – e.g. that there were a number of juniors waiting to be promoted or that the particular individual had supported the policy when applied to others.

Health and safety legitimate aims

Health and safety represents a separate category of legitimate aim to those discussed above. Such aims may be supported by statute. For example, it is Civil Aviation Authority policy that commercial pilots over 60 cannot fly solo. Further, international law is that pilots can only continue from 60-64 as part of a multi-pilot crew where the other pilot is under 60. This rule was challenged in ***Fries v Lufthansa CityLine GmbH*** [2017] IRLR 1003, ECJ. The ECJ found that there was a legitimate aim of establishing and maintaining a high uniform level of civil aviation safety. It took into account that Mr Fries could have continued working by training or examining pilots. It also took into account that the law did not prevent him from undertaking 'Ferry' or positioning flights, in which a plane is moved from one airport to another with no cargo or passengers.

If therefore it can be established that a certain level of physical fitness or capability is necessary for a role then health and safety legitimate aims may well be accepted. Of course, it will be necessary then to show that imposing a retirement age is proportionate, for example with evidence of age-related declining physical ability for the particular job, as was accepted in a non-retirement context in ***Wolf v Stadt Frankfurt am Main*** [2010] IRLR 244.

Proportionate means

Proportionality is addressed in the useful case of ***Pitcher v Chancellor, Masters and Scholars of the University of Oxford and another and Chancellor, Masters and Scholars of the University of Oxford v Ewart*** [2022] ICR 338, EAT. These two separate cases both looked at the application of a compulsory retirement age at Oxford University, known as the EJRA ('Employer Justified Retirement Age'). Both tribunals at first instance accepted legitimate aims of intergenerational fairness, facilitating succession planning and promoting equality and diversity. However, the tribunals came to opposing conclusions on proportionality. Prof Pitcher lost his case, whereas Prof Ewart won his.

The EAT was not disturbed by the diametrically opposed conclusions surrounding the same policy because neither tribunal had made an error of law. This was however not just an example of different tribunals coming to permissibly different conclusions on the same facts. There were also some material differences in the cases which led to different conclusions.

The main considerations used to reach the different conclusions were as follows:

Prof Pitcher:

- Expert on Shakespeare, working more in college.
- The tribunal had a survey which suggested that 25% of staff would have continued for a further 3 years absent the EJRA. It found that turnover would have been significantly lower were it not for the EJRA.
- The University successfully argued that the policy created a degree of predictability that would have been difficult to secure by other means (para 191).
- The fact that he was able to extend his employment past the EJRA (moving to a different fixed term post) mitigated the discriminatory effect of mandatory retirement.
- It was relevant that the fixed retirement age of 67 was the age most favoured in the consultation process undertaken before the EJRA was decided.
- Claim dismissed.

Prof Ewart:

- Physicist in a project team making more use of University facilities.

- He provided statistics to show that the EJRA only made a 2-4% increase in vacancy creation. The tribunal therefore found that this was not more than a marginal impact. The University had tried to argue that it was *Cockram*-obvious (i.e. so obvious that there was no need for evidence) that the compulsory retirement age helped to create vacancies at a faster rate, but the statistics helped to debunk this (para 185).

- The EAT also found (para 209) that it would have been open to the University to provide projections of what they expected to happen with vacancy creation if the policy was too new to have produced data (as was argued by the University).

- The fact that he was able to extend his employment past the EJRA (moving to a different fixed term post) did not sufficiently mitigate the discriminatory effect of mandatory retirement.

- Claim succeeded.

These cases show how statistical evidence can make a big difference to the outcome of claims. If Prof Pitcher had provided similar statistics to Prof Ewart, the result may have been different. It is often thought that only respondents provide statistics, but claimants can and should do the same if they are able.

At para 210, the EAT also noted that whether the PCP is a proportionate means of achieving a legitimate aim would have to be held under review – i.e. just because an ET has decided that a policy is justified does not mean it would necessarily do so 10 years down the line, as both evidence that the policy is working and circumstances may change.

<u>Relevance of pension provision to proportionality</u>

The nature of the employee's pension may be relevant in making decisions as to justification. Two cases at different ends of the judicial spectrum show that it can be taken into account as a way of mitigating the discriminatory effect of a retirement provision.

In ***Tilley and ors v Egyptair Airlines Co*** ET Case No.2207205/18, a mandatory retirement age of 65 was considered justified at ET level. The legitimate aims were intergenerational fairness and equality and dignity for retiring employees. The airline did not performance manage older employees, despite issues, as they were coming up to retirement. In determining proportionality, an important factor was a generous pension scheme.

In the ECJ case of ***Rosenbladt v Oellerking GmbH, Case C-45/09***, [2011] CMLR 1011, commercial cleaners were automatically terminated when they became entitled to retirement pension. The legitimate aims relied upon were – (1) sharing employment between the generations, making it easier for younger workers to find work, particularly in a time of chronic unemployment and (2) not requiring employers to dismiss older workers on grounds of incapacity, which may be humiliating. The court considered it a relevant factor that the rights of older workers were protected because their pensions served as replacement income. It held therefore that the legitimate aims were in principle capable of objectively and reasonably justifying a difference in treatment on grounds of age.

<u>Both the notion of compulsory retirement and the selected age need to be justified</u>

In ***Seldon,*** at EAT level ([2009] IRLR 267), Mr Justice Elias found that although the principle of compulsory retirement had been justified, the ET had erred in concluding that the specific retirement age of 65 was justified because performance would drop off at around that age (the '*dignity*' legitimate aim). The EAT found there was no evidence for this conclusion. It therefore remitted the case to the ET to decide whether the age of 65 was justified on the basis of the other two legitimate aims – staff retention and workforce planning.

In the Supreme Court, Lady Hale's analysis was that the EAT appeared to have accepted that the legitimate aims of staff retention and workforce planning could be met by any fixed retirement age (para 12). However, in her conclusion (para 68), she made clear that when the matter was remitted it might be important to consider whether the age of 65 could be justified in relation to those two legitimate aims. She essentially recommended that the ET unpicked the question of the age chosen and discussed it in relation to each objective.

In the end, the ET, on remittal did find that 65 was justified and the EAT backed it up – ***Seldon v Clarkson Wright and Jakes (No.2)*** [2014] ICR 1275, EAT.

The case reminds us that practitioners can sometimes be so caught up in looking at legitimate aims that the question of whether the same legitimate aims could be achieved with a higher retirement age can be overlooked. This is something that tribunals should look at carefully and it is therefore important that employers think about the reasoning behind the particular age, with evidence to back up any assertions.

Unfair Dismissal for retirement

Although the focus of this book is on discrimination law, there is a clear crossover with the law of unfair dismissal when it comes to retirement.

The test under s.98 Employment Rights Act 1996 is whether the employer acted reasonably in using retirement as the reason for dismissal; specifically, whether there was '*some other substantial reason for dismissal*' which was in the range of reasonable responses. This is *not* the same as whether the particular disadvantage is justified, however, it is highly likely that the two would go hand in hand. If dismissing at 67 for retirement was a proportionate means of achieving a legitimate aim, then the dismissal is extremely likely to be substantively fair (albeit it could be unfair for other reasons, such as procedure). The reverse is also true – if the dismissal is discriminatory, it is difficult to see how it could possibly be fair. This does not mean that tribunals should not apply each test separately – it would likely be an error of law not to do so.

How does an employer broach a conversation about retirement with an employee?

This can be complicated, but it can be done lawfully. We set out below a few guidelines, taken from case law and our own experience, as to how best to deal with this topic.

A conversation about retirement may stem from a need for workplace planning. It is generally not unreasonable for an employer to wish to know if an employee is thinking about leaving. An analogy may be made between this and asking a woman who has just announced her pregnancy how much maternity leave she is planning on taking. The question is not prohibited but must be asked in the right way.

Think about the reason for asking

An employer must carefully consider why it wants to know whether the employee will be retiring. The reason for asking must be capable of being justified.

As above, workplace planning may be cited as a reason to ask this question. However, any employee could leave at any point, subject to their notice requirements. The employer may have to justify why it needs to know the 65 year-old's plans further ahead than the notice period allows.

Another reason to broach retirement may be that performance is reducing and the employer wishes to avoid the ignominy of performance managing an employee who is coming to the end of their career. The preservation of dignity in such circumstances has been held to be a legitimate aim for retiring an employee (eg ***Seldon***) and therefore is certainly arguable as a legitimate aim for asking the question.

Employees who change their mind

In the case of ***Taylor v (1) Mane Limited (2) Jonathan Gray*** ET Case No. 2302987/2020, the claimant had been recruited before the change in the law on compulsory retirement and thus had a clause in her contract of employment which stated that the normal retirement age was 65. As she approached 65, the respondent asked her in neutral terms what her plans were for retirement. The tribunal accepted its evidence that it needed to know her plans for workplace planning reasons, given the niche nature of the perfume industry and the fact that it would take 6-12 months to recruit and train a replacement. There was therefore no less favourable treatment because of age.

The claimant said that she intended to retire at 65 because she felt expected to. The respondent understood this to mean that she would retire sometime in the 8 months after her 65th birthday. It therefore recruited a replacement at great cost. She did not in fact retire as expected as her intentions changed. Further, neutral conversations, occurred and eventually the claimant said she would retire just before her 67th birthday.

Meanwhile, her performance was becoming problematic. The claimant and the respondent had a conversation about retirement 3 months before her 67th birthday. By that point she had not given the 3 months' notice that the respondent had expected her to give. The respondent was concerned about the continuing cost of having recruited her replacement, paying two salaries. The tribunal found that this was another neutral conversation about retirement.

The claimant said she had been told that she 'owed' it to the respondent to retire and that it had given her a job at 60 when nobody else would have. This was not accepted by the tribunal, but if it had been would likely have constituted direct age discrimination or harassment.

She confirmed a month before her 67th birthday that she had no intention of retiring. This was accepted by the respondent and consequently, it made her replacement redundant. She did agree to retire just before her 68th birthday. She again changed her mind with no issue, volunteering to retire at 70. Around 6 months later she changed her mind. This was also accepted.

In the end, the claimant was dismissed fairly due to her performance about which the respondent continued to have concerns. There was no age discrimination.

It is noteworthy that in this case, the respondent did not hold the claimant to her previous intention to retire just before her 67th birthday and awaited her giving 3 months' notice as confirmation. Compare this to ***Green v Floorform*** (below) in which the claimant had given a date for retirement 18 months in advance and the respondent took this to be notice of retirement and did not allow the claimant to resile from it.

It is perhaps a useful lesson that once an employee has suggested that they wish to retire to ask them to agree a date.

When to do it

Clearly if there are issues with performance, then this may precipitate a conversation at a particular point in time. Employers should be careful not to assume that any performance issues have anything to do with age. However, in general, our view is that the longer the employer can wait, the more likely it is to be proportionate. There may be more force to the argument if an individual is asked to retire at state pension age (67 at present). It is also important to give good notice. Although employees will have notice periods, it is sensible to start discussions well in advance of a notice period and perhaps at least a year ahead.

How to approach the conversation

The more sensitive any conversation about retirement is, the more likely it will be held to be proportionate.

It is sensible to keep notes of such conversations or at least make a record by emailing a summary afterwards. It is not uncommon for there to be a dispute about exactly what was said or agreed or indeed if there was pressure applied or not.

In the ET case of ***Mr Richard Green v Floorform UK Ltd*** ET Case No: 2500745/2020, the claimant was a health and safety manager who had worked for the Respondent for over 30 years. The respondent became concerned that he may retire. He was crucial to the running of the company and the only health and safety officer. They wished to recruit another officer in good time before his retirement so that he could train that person up over a period of a year and ensure a good handover. There was evidence of this concern in board meeting minutes.

A director of the company approached the claimant in 2017 and asked him whether he had any plans for retirement. He said no and they agreed to touch base the following year. In 2018, a similar conversation occurred and the claimant said he would retire in 2020. As a result of this, the respondent recruited a new health and safety officer.

The claimant said that he had been pushed to commit to a date for retirement and also that he had said that it was provisional. The tribunal did not accept this evidence (notes would clearly have assisted) and found that he had agreed to retire in 18 months' time and that it was not open to him to subsequently unilaterally rescind that notice and continue working. His claims of unfair dismissal and age discrimination failed.

In ***Tapper v MoD*** ET Case Nos.1402660/2019 and 1400338/2020 the claimant was suffering health issues and was overloaded with work. He raised a grievance. Before the grievance was resolved, he was asked by management when he planned to retire. He was in his 60s. He had indicated no intention of wanting to retire or leave but simply wanted to have his workload reduced. The tribunal found (unsurprisingly) that someone in their 30s would not have been asked the same question.

The tribunal considered justification and held that although there existed genuine legitimate aims of effective management of staff and succession planning, these were not the aims in asking him whether he was going to retire. The motivation was because he had raised a grievance and it was an easy way of resolving matters. The tribunal found that it was unreasonable to ask him that question in circumstances where he in fact just wanted to know if his position was secure.

This case shows that context and timing can be very important in establishing whether a conversation about retirement is discriminatory or not. Further, that it is all very well citing the standard legitimate aims but they need to be shown to be the aims of the particular conversation under scrutiny.

Flexible retirement schemes

Pension schemes (such as the Local Government Pension Scheme or the NHS) may offer the opportunity to take flexible retirement. This concept usually entails that the employee draws some of their pension but continues to work on reduced pay – this may mean a reduction in seniority, a reduction in hours or both. The terms on which it can be done may vary from organisation to organisation.

In the ET case of ***Walker v London Borough of Lewisham*** ET Case No. 2301162/2020, the claimant claimed that not being allowed to return to full-time work some years after having taken flexible retirement was age discrimination (direct and indirect). The claims failed. The tribunal found that any PCP which was part of the flexible retirement policy would only apply to those over 55 years old. This meant that there could be no comparator pool of a different age group because the PCP could never apply to younger people.

The direct discrimination case failed for similar reasons – the claimant did not suffer less favourable treatment because of her age but because she had made a decision to accept flexible retirement (which had not been forced upon her).

In any event, the tribunal found that not allowing her to return to full-time work would be justified. The legitimate aims were intergenerational fairness, maximising performance and efficiency and succession planning. The tribunal recorded that the conduct was also proportionate because:

> '*The rationale is that more experienced, older members of staff will reduce their hours (or seniority) which facilitates the retention of knowledge within the organisation whilst allowing their skills and knowledge to be transferred to others, also aiding career development for employees. It also supports part time working opportunities for those over 55 who may be seeking to reduce their hours or commitment*'.

It is clear that the respondent provided good evidence of what its legitimate aims were but that the selection of the PCP meant that the claim could not even get off the ground. It appears likely that a claim based on the correct application of such a policy that an employee has voluntarily agreed to will make a claim for age discrimination difficult. If however the policy is not applied properly or the individual is pressured into applying, this may be a different matter.

CHAPTER EIGHT

PROVING AGE DISCRIMINATION

- *How much does a claimant have to prove before it is for the employer to disprove discrimination?*
- *How does a respondent discharge its burden of proof if it shifts?*
- *How can the choice of comparator assist to prove age discrimination?*
- *How can a respondent use a comparator to undermine a claim?*

The burden of proving age discrimination

The standard of proof in any case before the employment tribunal is "*on the balance of probabilities*". That means that in order to succeed on any particular point the tribunal only needs to be satisfied to this level, not "*beyond all reasonable doubt*" (as in criminal cases) or any more onerous standard. Tribunals are simply required to weigh the evidence and determine in whose favour the balance is tipped. Another way of describing this threshold is as a likelihood of 51%, compared to the criminal standard of proof which is sometimes said to be 99%. Both the judiciary and parliament have been mindful that it is rare for discrimination (especially direct discrimination) to be overt on the part of a discriminator, and it is therefore usually difficult for claimants to find evidence, documentary or other, which demonstrates direct discrimination – see ***Glasgow City Council v Zafar*** [1998] ICR 120, HL, per Lord Browne-Wilkinson. For that reason, the burden of proof in discrimination cases is assessed in two stages and is therefore not only on the claimant, as it would be, for example, in a contractual claim where the claimant must prove the breach on the balance of probabilities.

Section 136 Equality Act 2010 ('EqA') relevantly sets out:

> *Burden of proof*
>
> *(1) This section applies to any proceedings relating to a contravention of this Act.*
>
> *(2) If there are facts from which the court could decide, in the absence of any other explanation, that a person (A) contravened the provision concerned, the court must hold that the contravention occurred.*
>
> *(3) But subsection (2) does not apply if A shows that A did not contravene the provision.*

Stage 1 – a *prima facie* case – s.136(2) EqA

Essentially, once a claimant proves facts from which the tribunal could conclude, in the absence of any other explanation, that an employer has committed an act of direct discrimination, the tribunal is obliged to uphold the claim unless the employer can show that it did not discriminate. This is described by lawyers as establishing a *prima facie* case, but has been colloquially described as, "*giving the tribunal something to hang the allegation of discrimination on*"; and/or a requirement that the claimant needs to "*show something a bit suspicious in relation to the protected characteristic*", without requiring the claimant to demonstrate that they have been discriminated against.

Although the burden of proof provisions in the EqA aim to assist claimants, the primary burden still lies with the claimant. Tribunals and courts have been at pains to remind claimants that they do have to show something to indicate that discrimination might have happened, as opposed to just unfavourable or less favourable treatment. Lord Justice Mummery in ***Madarassy v Nomura International plc*** [2007] ICR 867, CA, stated (para.56):

> *"(T)he bare facts of a difference in status and a difference in treatment only indicate a possibility of discrimination. They are not, without more, sufficient material from which a tribunal "could conclude" that, on the balance of probabilities, the respondent had committed an unlawful act of discrimination".*

<u>The burden of proof in direct age discrimination cases</u>

Once a *prima facie* case has been established, the burden of proof shifts to the respondent to demonstrate, again on the balance of probabilities, that it did not discriminate.

It is impossible to list all the circumstances in which the burden of proof can be shifted on to the respondent in a direct age discrimination case. The Supreme Court in ***Efobi v Royal Mail Group Ltd*** [2021] ICR 1263, SC, made clear that the tribunal could consider evidence from all sources at stage one, including evidence from the respondent aiming to rebut the allegation of discrimination, though the respondent's explanation for the conduct should be ignored until stage 2.

<u>Examples of circumstances in which the burden of proof might shift to the respondent</u>

Unreasonable conduct on the part of an employer is not sufficient on its own to establish discrimination, but it may be evidence supporting that inference if there is nothing else to explain the behaviour — ***Anya v University of Oxford and anor*** [2001] ICR 847, CA. There is a valid "*bastard defence*", well-known to employment lawyers, more delicately described as being "*unreasonable not discriminatory*". This means that an employer might have treated an employee badly, but if they treat everyone equally badly, they are not discriminating against anyone. This is likely to be harder to demonstrate, though not impossible, in a case where the evidence shows that only one employee was subjected to the employer's unreasonable behaviour — see ***Kowalewska-Zietek v Lancashire Teaching Hospitals NHS Foundation Trust*** EAT 0269/15. In that case, the claimant was a Polish hospital consultant whose clinical competence had been questioned. The hospital demonstrated that the complaints about her were partly due to administrative errors and its actions towards her would have occurred regardless of her nationality/race. Mr Justice Langstaff stated in obiter comments (para.48):

> *"Where there is an approach towards all which creates an equality of misery it is particularly clear that it is unlikely to be because of a protected characteristic peculiar to only one or a few of them. However the "unreasonable not discriminatory" defence may be less applicable in a case in which the evidence shows that only one employee has in particular been made miserable. In that latter case, though it remains logically right that the individual may have been the unwilling victim of a mistake or oversight, there is much greater reason to consider carefully and with particular scrutiny whether this might simply be too easy an explanation."*

If there has been a failure to follow procedures set down by a company policy or a statutory Code of Practice (like the EHRC Employment Code) for someone of a different age to others (for whom the policy or Code was or would likely be followed), that failure might be enough to shift the burden on to the respondent (see ***Anya,*** as above).

If the claimant shows herself to have been treated less favourably than differently-aged people, by someone who historically made a comment in relation to age, that might discharge the claimant's burden of proof. Take the example of a much older employee who is passed over for promotion, despite younger colleagues, with lesser experience and qualifications, being promoted. If the manager making the promotion decisions had once called the older employee "*Grandad*", even if the name-calling was historic, not an allegation in the claim and/or it occurred outside of the limitation period, such a comment could nevertheless assist the claimant to shift the burden, requiring the respondent to show that age had nothing whatsoever to do with the decision not to promote – see ***London Borough of Ealing v Rihal*** [2004] IRLR 642, CA. In the ***Rihal*** case, the Court of Appeal emphasised the appropriateness of looking at the wider picture in deciding whether the protected characteristic was a factor which explained particular adverse treatment.

Evidence of a purported discriminator having a history of allegedly treating older or younger people more favourably might be helpful to show a propensity for certain discriminatory conduct. For example, if a claimant claims that the reason their application for a certain role was rejected was that the decision-maker did not want to appoint someone young to the role, and there is evidence of the same decision-maker having a grievance upheld against them from a candidate for a different role who complained that they were not appointed because of their tender age, the evidence of the upheld grievance might assist the claimant to shift the burden of proof.

Sometimes statistics about the demographics of those more or less favourably treated might be sufficient to shift the burden. For example, in a redundancy selection exercise, even without any of the selection criteria exposing a blatant preference for younger candidates, if 90% of the employees selected for redundancy are under the age of 30 years, whereas only 30% of the pool of employees at risk of redundancy are under that age, the tribunal might be willing to shift the burden onto the Respondent.

The *question and answer* process

One way a claimant may be assisted in gathering evidence of this nature is through the "*ask and respond*" process. The process is designed to enable claimants, or prospective claimants, to understand the reasons for the decisions they wish to challenge, but it can also provide persuasive evidence to an employment tribunal, or assist in shifting the burden of proof to the respondent in a discrimination case. The following ACAS Guidance might be of assistance:

https://www.acas.org.uk/asking-and-answering-questions-about-discrimination

The prospective claimant should prepare a statement, giving details of the allegations and the reasons why it is alleged they amount to age discrimination, and ask whether the employer agrees with the account and if not, why not. Other questions to ask in an age discrimination context, for example, in a promotion case, might include:

- What were the ages of those people who applied for the position I applied for?
- What were the ages of those people who were appointed to the position I applied for?
- What are the age statistics of particular levels of management?
- What ages were those who made the decision not to accept my application?
- What policies does the employer have, for example on recruitment or equality and diversity, and do the policies have any information on training for managers in relation to age discrimination in particular?
- What number of people within a certain age bracket (specify the relevant age bracket(s)) have been recruited/promoted in the last 5 years?
- What number of people within the comparator age bracket (specify the comparator age bracket) have been recruited/promoted in the last 5 years?

Although it is not legally obligatory for an employer to respond, if an employer does not respond, or gives different answers in a tribunal hearing, adverse inferences could be drawn by the tribunal, where such an inference is appropriate, see ***D'Silva v NATFHE (now University and***

College Union) [2008] IRLR 412, EAT). This might also assist a claimant to shift the burden to the respondent.

Shifting the burden of proof for other forms of age discrimination

Section 136 EqA applies to all forms of discrimination under the EqA, not just direct discrimination. In relation to harassment, the claimant needs to prove there was unwanted conduct which had the prescribed purpose or effect under s.26. Although the claimant need not prove that it was related to age, they would need to give some indication on the evidence that age was relevant somehow, before the burden is likely to shift. In ***Bell v Scorpion Engineering Ltd*** ET Case No.1401065/07, the claimant argued that she had been subjected to “bossy and overbearing” treatment from her foreman, related to the fact she was the youngest person in the company, and this was therefore age-related harassment. The tribunal found that the foreman was no more bossy towards the claimant than he was to other employees and therefore the treatment had not been shown to be related to age and the burden did not shift to the respondent.

In relation to indirect discrimination, it is for the claimant to prove a PCP which placed or would place the claimant and people of the same or similar age at a particular disadvantage (s.19(2)(a) – (c) EqA), but it is for the respondent to prove that the PCP was objectively justified (s.19(2)(d) EqA).

For victimisation, generally the claimant will have to establish more than the protected act and the detriment. A claimant will need to give some evidence to suggest that there was a causal link between the protected act and the detriment, but will not be required to prove causation on the balance of probabilities. Sometimes it will be enough to show that either the detriment occurred shortly after the protected act or that a detrimental decision-maker was shown to be disgruntled about the protected act or that those who had not done a protected act were treated differently.

Stage 2 – Providing a non-discriminatory explanation – s.136(3) EqA

If the burden of proof is found to have passed to a respondent and the respondent then fails to give an explanation, or is not believed, the discrimination will be upheld. If the respondent gives an explanation for the treatment the tribunal need do no more than to say it was not persuaded that it was genuinely the explanation, rather than to reject the explanation given by the respondent and suggest what the real explanation was.

In ***Martin v British Car Auctions Limited*** ET Case No. 2407168/2021, although the ET found that the person deciding on the redundancy selection was not consciously motivated by the claimant's age, they found that a younger colleague was more favourably treated and there was no material difference in terms of skills and qualification. The ET found that the burden had shifted to the employer, and it had failed to explain adequately why the claimant had been selected. The tribunal therefore upheld the claim that the dismissal was tainted with age discrimination.

In ***Canadian Imperial Bank of Commerce v Beck*** EAT 0141/10 a Head of Department, who was considered by the tribunal to be best placed to rebut the inference of discrimination, had not been called as a witness. The claimant had satisfied the tribunal of facts from which age discrimination could be inferred, and the tribunal could not be sure of whether the redundancy was influenced by age because they had not heard from the witness. The age discrimination claim was upheld.

It matters not if a respondent gives an unreasonable explanation or one which exposes incompetence on its behalf, if the tribunal is satisfied it is not discriminatory then it could be enough to discharge the respondent's burden of proof and the discrimination claim will be dismissed. Even if the respondent accepts that the redundancy selection exercise was a *dog's dinner*, if the tribunal are nevertheless satisfied that age was not the reason for the mess, then the burden will be discharged – see ***Osoba v Chief Constable of Hertfordshire Constabulary*** EAT 0055/13. Nevertheless, tribunals will be alert to a respondent seeking to hide a more sinister motivation under a cloak of contrived incompetence. Once the burden of proof has shifted, the respondent is on the back foot with the tribunal and should strive to provide a satisfactory explanation which is entirely unrelated to age.

A difficult situation can occur when the respondent denies that the alleged discriminatory act occurred as a matter of fact. For example, an allegation that a manager was physically aggressive. If the witness claims that the incident did not occur, it is impossible for him to provide any sort of explanation for something that he did not do. This means that if the tribunal finds that he did do it and there is some other context which shifts the burden, the claim will inevitably be upheld as no non-discriminatory explanation can be given. In such circumstances, a respondent witness would be well advised to provide general evidence of how his decision-making and actions are never affected by age. This may stop the burden from being shifted in the first place or convince the tribunal that none of the manager's acts would be influenced by age.

Flexibility nevertheless required on approach to burden of proof

Although there is quite a lot of case law on the shifting burden of proof, the courts have been relatively consistent in stating that strict, mechanical application of the rule under s.136 is not required in every case, and it may even be confusing to decision-making if such an approach is adopted. Sometimes, particularly where a tribunal has made positive findings on causation, reference to the shifting burden of proof is simply unnecessary. In ***Gay v Sophos plc*** EAT 0452/10, the tribunal found that a 55-year-old claimant was made redundant and placed on garden leave. She was not considered for alternative roles, unlike her younger colleagues, but the tribunal concluded that the employer thought she would not have been interested in more junior roles with lower pay and therefore age was not a factor in why she was not offered suitable alternative employment. The EAT found there was no need for the tribunal to go through the stages under s.136. It was clear that discrimination had not been made out.

Comparators

Choosing a comparator

The choice of comparator (see Chapter 2 Direct age discrimination) can be crucial in proving age discrimination. Usually a claimant is required to identify a comparator (actual and/or hypothetical), if not already identified in the pleadings, at a preliminary stage in tribunal proceedings. It is important that some careful thought be devoted to this.

The EqA defines age as a person of a particular age, or belonging to an 'age group'. The law does not say how wide an age group is, but the ACAS guidance on age discrimination makes clear it can be quite wide, for example the under 20s or over 50s. Terms such as 'Gen Z' or 'millennials' can also indicate an age group. Any claimant claiming age discrimination will need to be specific about their age (either being a particular age or an age group) being causative of the treatment complained of in a direct discrimination case (or being causative of the disadvantage caused by a PCP in an indirect discrimination case – see Chapter 3 Indirect age discrimination). The comparator (actual or hypothetical) is similarly either a particular age or of a particular age group which is different to the claimant's, and was more favourably treated (or not disadvantaged by a PCP).

In general, it is more difficult to prove less favourable treatment because of a slight age difference than because of a substantial difference. The EAT have endorsed strike out, where the difference in age between the claimant and the comparator was only nine months, on the basis that prospects of success of demonstrating facts from which discrimination could be inferred were "*fanciful*" – ***ABN AMRO Management Services Ltd and anor v Hogben*** EAT 0266/09. The exception is a case which concerns a cut-off age or a specific age, e.g. a benefit only available to those younger than 18 years or to those who have reached state pension age, or to people of a certain age and no-one else, like a bonus payment on 50th birthdays, but no bonus at any other age. In these cases a difference of a day to an age could mean more or less favourable treatment (see ***Citibank NA and ors v Kirk*** [2022] EAT 103). In a non-cut-off case, it is generally more persuasive to have a comparator with a significant difference in age. For example, in relation to an allegation that C-suite executives are only recruited from the candidates who are over 50 years old, a 32-year-old claimant is more likely to be successful in a direct age discrimination complaint than a similarly qualified 49-year-old claimant, because a tribunal is more likely to be persuaded that a significant age difference was at least part of the reason for the refusal to promote.

Comparators in group litigation

In group litigation, the comparator needs to be identified very carefully, and often the "*ask and respond*" procedure (see above) can be deployed early in the litigation to assist with identifying the comparator. The statistics might show that, despite suspicions on the part of the claimants, there is no evidence of different treatment until there is a large difference in ages, or there appears to be a bias against one age group but not another.

All claimants in the group claiming age discrimination need to be included within the age group (or groups) specified. It is often, in large groups, worth pleading alternative age groups. For example, if the group of age discrimination claimants are aged between 38 and 55 years, the less favourable treatment could be pleaded as less favourable treatment of those aged above 38 years compared to those aged 37 years and younger; alternatively, of those aged above 45 years compared to those aged 37 years and younger; alternatively, of those aged over 50 years compared to those aged 37 years and younger. Of course, if the last alternative argument succeeds, then only those over the age of 50 years will succeed in their claim, but this is overall a better result than the very wide age groups which are very close together, diluting the strength of all of the claims. Without the alternative age groups being pleaded, a canny respondent could adduce evidence of lots of employees aged 38 to 40 years who were afforded better treatment than the claimants, and this evidence could undermine the claims of less favourable treatment of those aged 38 and above; those claimants aged over 50 years old in this example, would also be unsuccessful. For this reason, if there is only one claimant in a large group who is aged under, say, 50 years, and that person is significantly younger, say, 38 years, it is sometimes worthwhile persuading that claimant to withdraw the claim to increase the prospects of those above the age of 50 years who can claim based on a more substantial age differential with the comparator group.

How can a respondent use comparator evidence in its favour?

To rebut the discrimination allegation, a respondent would be well advised to find an actual comparator, if at all possible, in the same age group as the claimant has specified, who was comparatively well treated; or a comparator in a different age group who was similarly badly treated, in order to undermine any inference of discrimination. If a statutory comparator (where there is no material difference between the comparator's circumstances and the claimant's, apart from age – see s.23(1) EqA) cannot be found, a respondent can lead evidence of how a comparator who was in similar but not identical circumstances (an "evidential comparator" – see Chapter 2 Direct age discrimination) was treated. This can be powerful evidence in the respondent's favour. Again, a respondent would be well advised to consider the claimant and comparator groups very carefully when identified by the claimant, and scrutinise the available data to determine whether there are any actual statutory or evidential comparators to undermine the claims.

CHAPTER NINE

REMEDIES

- *Declarations and Recommendations*
- *Financial loss*
- *Mitigation*
- *Polkey-style Reductions*
- *Injury to feelings*
- *Aggravated Damages*
- *Exemplary Damages*
- *Personal Injury*
- *Accelerated Receipt*
- *ACAS Uplift*
- *Interest*
- *Tax and Grossing Up*
- *Order of Adjustments*

If the tribunal finds in a claimant's favour on liability in an age discrimination claim, they can award one or more of the following three remedies:

(a) A declaration as to the rights of the claimant, under section 124(2)(a) Equality Act 2010 ('EqA');

(b) Compensation under section 124(2)(b) EqA;

(c) An appropriate recommendation under section 124(2)(c);

Depending on the type of discrimination that has been established, the tribunal may have to consider remedies other than compensation first. If the tribunal have found that indirect discrimination took place, and they are '*satisfied that the provision, criterion, or practice was not applied with the intention of discrimination against the complainant*' then the tribunal must consider whether to make a declaration or recommendation first, before they consider whether to order compensation – s124(4) and (5). This obligation does not mean that compensation is not awarded in cases of unintentional indirect discrimination – it often is.

Declarations

Section 124(2)(a) EqA sets out that a declaration is one of the formal remedies available to a claimant who has succeeded on their claim for age discrimination.

A declaration is a formal statement made by the tribunal confirming that discrimination has occurred. A declaration can be made alongside other remedies, but it can also be made on its own where no financial loss has been suffered. It is rare that a claimant will solely seek a declaration. However, this may sometimes be the case where a claimant has pursued a case of age discrimination on a point of principle and where there has been no financial loss.

A declaration can often be as simple as '*by failing to appoint the claimant to the role of deputy head, the respondent discriminated against the claimant because of her age*'.

Recommendations

Section 124(2)(c) Equality Act 2010 sets out that a tribunal may '*make an appropriate recommendation.*' Section 124(3) sets out that "*appropriate recommendation*" refers to a '*recommendation that within a specified period the respondent takes specified steps for the purpose of obviating or reducing the adverse effect on the complainant of any matter to which proceedings relate.*' If the employer does not comply with the recommendation without a reasonable excuse, the tribunal may increase the compensatory award that they have made or, if no such award was made, they can make one (s.124(2)(b) and s.124(7)).

It is important to note that since 2015, recommendations can no longer be made that would require an employer to take steps for the purpose of reducing the adverse effect on "*any other person*". This means that any recommendation must relate to reducing the adverse effect specifically on the claimant. If the claimant has been dismissed and is no longer employed by the respondent, it is therefore unlikely that there will be much scope for an appropriate recommendation.

Examples of recommendations could be:

- That the senior management team attend training on age discrimination within 3 months (in order to reduce the likelihood of future acts of age related harassment against the claimant);

- That the recruitment policy is amended within a month to comply with equality legislation (if the tribunal has found the policy to be indirectly discriminatory to those under 30 so that the claimant can reapply).

Compensation – Financial Loss

The most common remedy sought, and the subject of most remedy hearings, is compensation. Significantly, unlike some other common employment tribunal claims brought under the Employment Rights Act

1996, there is no statutory cap or upper limit on the compensatory award that a tribunal can make under the Equality Act 2010.

A tribunal has a discretion to award compensation if it is '*just and equitable to do so*'- ***Hurley v Mustoe (No 2)*** [1983] ICR 422, EAT. Once it makes the election to award compensation, the actual amount of compensation is not subject to a '*just and equitable*' test, unlike compensation for unfair dismissal. Indeed, the test is that '*as best as money can do it, the applicant must be put into the position she [or he] would have been in but for the unlawful conduct*' (***Ministry of Defence v Cannock and ors*** [1994] ICR 918 EAT). The purpose of compensation is not to punish the respondent but to compensate the claimant. It therefore follows that any loss must have a causal link to the particular act of discrimination.

Although discrimination is often treated as similar to other torts, it should be noted that there is no requirement of reasonable foreseeability, at least in claims of direct discrimination and harassment – ***Essa v Laing Ltd*** [2004] IRLR 313. This means that as long as a causal link is established, a claimant can recover their losses. There is no clear authority on the question of whether loss arising from indirect discrimination must be reasonably foreseeable.

There are a number of issues relevant to pecuniary loss, otherwise known as financial loss:

- Loss of earnings
- Loss of bonus
- Loss of benefits
- Pension loss
- Whole career loss

- Stigma damages

Loss of earnings

The most obvious and common form of pecuniary loss is loss of earnings following dismissal. Claimants who have been dismissed can claim for the difference between what they would have earned had the discrimination not occurred, i.e. had they not been dismissed, and what they actually did earn. This is subject to one, major, caveat which is the duty to mitigate. In practice, this means being obliged to look for another job at similar remuneration to the one that was lost (see 'duty to mitigate' below).

Claimants will have to provide a schedule of loss which sets out what they would have earned had the discrimination not taken place. This should be their net salary (i.e. take home pay). Template schedules of loss are available online. Claimants will also need to declare what money they have earned over that period and offset that against what is being claimed. For example, if an individual has been dismissed discriminatorily and gets a new job after three months of unemployment at the same or higher salary then they can claim for three months' losses (subject to any arguments on mitigation). If the new job is at a lower salary, then they may be able to claim for three months' full pay, followed by a reasonable period for which they will be awarded the difference between the old and new salaries.

When loss of earnings is claimed, it should be split into past loss (i.e. before the date of the tribunal hearing) and future loss. Past loss is generally easier to claim than future loss as it has already occurred, whereas there is a strong element of speculation in future loss involving a prediction of when the claimant is likely to get a new job. It should be noted however that just because past loss has already occurred does not prevent a tribunal from refusing to award those losses if a claimant has failed to mitigate.

In terms of how much future loss should be awarded, the tribunal should award losses up until the claimant is more likely than not to find alternative employment at the same salary. The case of ***Wardle v Credit Agricole Corporate and Investment Bank*** [2011] ICR 1290 found that it will be an error of law to award losses until the tribunal is absolutely sure that the claimant will get a new job. For example, it would be wrong to find that a claimant is entitled to full losses for two years, after which there is a 70% chance that he will get a new job such he is entitled to 30% of his losses for another 2 years, at which point he will definitely get a new job such that losses stop. The reason behind this guidance is that predicting when someone will get a new job inevitably involves a guess – the tribunal might overestimate or underestimate. Therefore, choosing the point at which the claimant is more likely than not to get a new job (i.e. a 51% chance) is the tribunal's best guess for when losses should end.

We note however that percentage predictions are perfectly proper when assessing the chances of what would have happened had the claimant stayed employed. For example, in assessing what a claimant's financial losses are, tribunals must consider whether employees would have increased their salary had they remained employed. This may be through predictable annual pay rises which would have definitely happened, or promotions which may have happened. In the latter category, a tribunal will decide, on the basis of evidence, what the percentage chance of promotion is. If the chance is 50%, it can award losses based on half the lower salary plus half the higher salary. We further note that in ***MOD v Cannock and ors*** [1994] IRLR 509, the EAT warned that tribunals should be careful of assessing the chance of promotion on the high side (para 140). See section below on *Polkey*-style reductions for more on these type of calculations.

Loss of bonus

If the claimant has evidence that a bonus would have been paid during the period of losses, this can also be claimed. Respondents will often argue that because the bonus is discretionary, the bonus would not have or may not have been paid. Tribunals will look at the evidence to decide what the likelihood of a bonus being paid is. This may include information about what bonuses were received by the claimant in the past and what bonuses were in fact received by colleagues in similar positions after she left. As above, it is open to the tribunal to find that there was a percentage chance of a bonus being paid and therefore award a proportion of the value of the bonus.

Loss of benefits

Earnings are not the only losses to which a victim of discrimination may be entitled. Any benefits such as gym membership, personal use of a company car and health insurance can be quantified and claimed for the period that they are lost. If they are taxable benefits, it is the net loss which is recoverable. The same applies for share options, albeit this may involve more complex calculations.

Pension Loss

A key element of remedy for dismissal claims concerning age discrimination is likely to be pension loss. This can be difficult to calculate and is therefore often put to one side at the early stages of claims. We strongly recommend that minds are turned to pension loss as early as possible if the claimant is in a defined benefit, final salary or career average pension scheme, as a claim for pension losses can dwarf any other element of the claim. These schemes are often applicable to public sector employees.

The guidelines for pension loss are set out in the extremely helpful 'Employment Tribunals – Principles for Compensation Pension Loss', updated most recently in March 2021.

https://www.judiciary.uk/wp-content/uploads/2013/08/Principles-Third-Revision-2021.pdf

There are usually considered to be two ways of calculating pension loss. The first of these is the contributions method, which is appropriate for most cases and involves a simple calculation of what employer contributions have been lost. The second method is the seven-step model, which will be required to calculate pension loss in more complex cases where there is a long period of ongoing loss, most commonly public sector cases. This will involve obtaining predictions of what the annual pension would have been and comparing it to what the claimant will actually receive on retirement (including any pension obtained by way of mitigation). That provides a figure for annual loss which is then multiplied by the appropriate figure for the claimant taken from the Ogden tables.

Other approaches can be used if supported by expert evidence. If a departure is justified, tribunals are not bound to follow the presidential guidance.

A further pension-related loss may occur if, as a result of a discriminatory dismissal, a claimant accesses their pension early. This may occur if the claimant is not able to obtain a new job and therefore needs to draw down pension funds earlier than expected in order to supplement their income. If the claimant can show that they would not have taken those steps if they had not been subject to discrimination, then in principle any reduction in value of the overall pension fund (e.g. penalties for early access) is a loss arising from the discrimination and is claimable. As always, this will be subject to the duty to mitigate and so claimants will be expected to choose a reasonable option and perhaps will be expected to take financial advice. Calculations can be fiendish and it is likely a report from an actuary will be necessary in complex or high value cases.

Non-dismissal claims

Loss of earnings may also be claimed for those who have not been dismissed, in specific cases. For example, if an employee has not been paid a bonus, given a pay rise or promoted due to their age, they may be able to claim the difference between their actual salary and the salary they would have received had they been promoted. However, it should be noted that just because an individual was subject to discrimination in the promotion process (i.e. age was taken into account in the decision), this does not mean that they definitely would have been promoted. As above, a tribunal will base compensation on what the chance of promotion would have been, absent any discrimination.

If a claimant is off work sick, but still employed, as a result of a discriminatory act and has a loss of earnings as a result, the difference between sick pay and normal pay may also be claimed.

Career loss

In rare cases, a claimant may argue that they are never going to be able to get a job of the same level again. This is called whole career loss. It can occur when a serious act of discrimination leads to psychiatric injury that means an individual is no longer able to work in their chosen career. Or if the nature of the claim was so public that the claimant will struggle to be accepted back into the industry. ***Wardle v Credit Agricole Corporate and Investment Bank*** [2011] ICR 1290 offers guidelines for this sort of case. See the sections below on mitigation and stigma damages for other examples where damages have been awarded to retirement.

In making a career loss award, the tribunal ought to take into account the '*vicissitudes of life*' i.e. the percentage chance that the claimant would have resigned, been fairly dismissed or would have had their career cut short for some other reason. This is generally a relatively small reduction.

Stigma damages

Chagger v Abbey National plc [2010] ICR 397 is the main authority for the concept of stigma damages in discrimination cases. In that case, Mr Chagger argued that the fact that he had brought his claim against Abbey National would put off future employers in the same industry from recruiting him. There was a stigma attached to him as some sort of troublemaker. He argued that his extensive attempts showed that he would never get another job in banking, so he changed careers and as a result was paid much less. The Court accepted that stigma damages were recoverable, notwithstanding the fact that the employers who refused to recruit him could also be subject to a claim of victimisation. However, there has to be compelling evidence that the employee is unlikely ever to be employed again in that industry.

The Court noted that if indeed there is good evidence to show that an individual will be unable to find an equivalent job, despite reasonable attempts at mitigation, then it does not really matter whether it is due to stigma or some other reason (para 98). The claimant is still entitled to compensation flowing from that difficulty, as the employer put him in that position to start with.

Finally, Elias LJ noted one unusual circumstance worthy of mention. If an employer can show that a dismissed employee would have been dismissed anyway (e.g. due to redundancy) but the facts show that because of stigma, that employee cannot get a new job, then a tribunal will have to assess the losses arising from the stigma. This will involve the difficult task of separating it out from the other reasons why the employee cannot find a new job and quantifying it, perhaps with a modest lump sum, or if the evidence is more conclusive, an award for future loss (para 99).

Adjustments to compensation

Respondents have a number of arguments at their disposition when seeking to minimise the compensation payable to claimants as follows:

- Failure to mitigate losses
- *Polkey*-style reductions
- Contributory fault (albeit this is unlikely to succeed)

Duty to mitigate

As with a claim for unfair dismissal brought under the Employment Rights Act 1996, claimants have a duty to take reasonable steps to mitigate their loss. This most often comes up in cases of dismissal. The main question for the tribunal will be whether the claimant has appropriately mitigated their loss by securing or reasonably attempting to secure new employment.

Any earnings or other benefits received by way of mitigation will be deducted from the claimant's financial losses as otherwise the claimant would receive a windfall. If the claimant has not taken reasonable steps to mitigate their loss, then a tribunal will deduct the sums that the claimant should have received by way of mitigation.

The burden lies with the employer to prove that the claimant has failed to mitigate their loss. The EAT provided useful mitigation guidelines in ***Cooper Contracting Ltd. v Lindsay*** UKEAT/0184/15, holding that '*a Claimant does not have to prove he has mitigated his loss*' and '*what has to be proved is that the Claimant acted unreasonably; he does not have to show that what he did was reasonable*'. Indeed, if an employer seeks to argue that the claimant has not taken reasonable steps, it is for them to provide evidence that there was a failure to mitigate. While the burden of proof does lie with employers, if a claimant has made multiple job applications or has struggled to find any suitable job adverts, it is highly recommended that they provide evidence of the steps they have taken. This may take the form of applications and rejections and screenshots of job searches.

Similarly, respondents are strongly advised to provide evidence to show that jobs were available for which the claimant did not apply. Ideally this evidence should be contemporaneous such that ideally, the respondent should start saving the results for job searches as soon a claim is received. If this is not possible, then non-contemporaneous evidence may be accepted as showing the approximate state of the job market. Such jobs should involve reasonable travel time for the claimant and have similar pay, responsibility and benefits to the former job.

In ***Hibiscus Housing Association Ltd v McIntosh Ltd*** [2009] 7 WLUK 579 (para.11), the EAT highlighted that the duty to take reasonable steps to mitigate does not mean that a claimant is necessarily expected to take any possible employment or the first job they are offered. This is particularly the case for senior employees. The EAT held that *'a dismissed manager, for example, may be able to work as a cleaner, but it is not reasonable to expect him or her to do so immediately. It may become reasonable to expect the dismissed employee to accept a lesser paid job with lesser status after a period of time, but that is a matter of fact and degree for the tribunal.'* This will be relevant in age discrimination claims where older, senior members of staff have been dismissed.

An employee failing to look for any jobs at all is likely to be sufficient to discharge the employer's burden of proof. It is then for the claimant to explain why such a failure was reasonable. In ***Hilco Capital Ltd v Harrington*** [2022] EAT 156, the EAT observed:

> *'Where [an] employee has simply made no job applications at all, the employer is entitled to assert, at least as a starting point, that by failing to do so, she has acted unreasonably, subject to the tribunal being satisfied as to the explanation.'*

Claimants can mitigate their loss through means other than securing new employment. In some cases, it may be considered reasonable for a claimant to mitigate their loss by retraining into a new profession. Whether the decision to retrain is considered reasonable will be highly fact specific. However, the tribunal is likely to take into account what the claimant's employment prospects were without retraining, for how long the claimant had previously been attempting to secure employment before deciding to retrain, the circumstances of the dismissal and whether there are any other factors that make it difficult for the claimant to obtain employment in their old field, for example, the respondent's refusal to provide a reference.

In age discrimination cases on behalf of older claimants, one common argument regarding mitigation is the increased difficulty facing older applicants for new jobs. For the period up until the tribunal hearing, this will simply be demonstrated by the fact that the claimant does not have a new job, despite having taken reasonable steps to mitigate their loss. However, with regard to future loss, it may be appropriate to argue that a claimant above (say) 60 in a specialist field may struggle to get any other job before her desired retirement age. Depending on how long the claimant has already remained unemployed, the tribunal may accept that she is unlikely to get a job before the end of her career. It may be sensible for claimants to obtain statistics if at all possible – for example, the website www.diversityintech.co.uk provides links to surveys and statistics about ageism in the technology industry. Recruiters such as Hays and totaljobs.com commission their own surveys on ageism in recruitment and the Centre for Ageing Better also produces some useful resources. Similarly, respondents wishing to rebut such arguments may wish to obtain their own statistics. If the sums claimed are significant, a career expert may even need to be instructed.

In the case of ***Gregory v Petro Trace Ltd*** ET Case No. 3304188/2022, a 62 year-old geophysicist was subject to age discrimination when he was dismissed due to a desire to '*bring in younger and more active experts*' and an assumption that because he was in his sixties, he had money. The tribunal found that given his niche field, and his long career in the industry, it was not unreasonable for him to be looking for an opportunity commensurate with his skills and experience, something he was struggling to find. It therefore awarded him his full losses to retirement at 66, finding that he would have worked part-time for the last year.

'*Polkey*'-style reductions

The well-known principle of *Polkey* (from the landmark case of ***Polkey v AE Dayton Services Ltd*** [1987] UKHL 8) is often applied in unfair dismissal cases where a tribunal decides that there was an unfair dismissal but that the claimant would have been dismissed fairly in any event after a certain period. Any pecuniary award is therefore limited to that period. Alternatively, the tribunal might decide that there was a percentage chance that the claimant would have been fairly dismissed in any event. A combination of these two options can also occur. For example, a tribunal could find that the claimant would have had a 50% chance of being dismissed in a redundancy exercise three months after the unfair dismissal took place and another 50% chance of being dismissed six months following that, in a second redundancy exercise. This would mean that (subject to mitigation) the claimant would receive three months' full losses, six months of 50% losses and any losses after nine months would be at 25%.

The question what would have happened '*but for*' the discrimination – is a perennial issue in tort cases. It was of no surprise therefore that the Court of Appeal in ***Chagger v Abbey National plc*** [2010] ICR 397 confirmed that the question of *Polkey* should be asked in discrimination cases. The process is the same and therefore compensation should be discounted either by a percentage reduction, a defined period of compensation or a combination of the two.

The Court warned (paras 69-72) that tribunals should avoid finding that losses should stop at a certain point on the basis that the claimant would have moved on to a new job anyway had he remained employed. This would not be a just measure of damages as it ignores the fact that the discriminatory dismissal put the claimant onto the labour market at a time not of his choosing and meant that he was looking for a job whilst being unemployed, something that makes it more difficult to find a new job. In other words, if the only reason the employee would have left was to move to an equivalent or better job, then his compensation should continue until he finds an equivalent or better job, even if that is a longer period than the period he would have stayed employed had there been no discrimination. This is subject, of course, to reasonable mitigation.

Examples of the *Polkey*-style reductions that might be made, at any percentage up to and including 100% after a certain date, are as follows:

- Claimant would have been made redundant;

- Claimant had plans to retire in any event;
- Claimant would have reduced to part-time (in which case any continuing losses are at the lower salary);
- Claimant would have been dismissed fairly and non-discriminatorily (for example for capability or misconduct reasons).

It should be noted that in relation to a hypothetical conduct dismissal, the tribunal can only take into account matters that occurred before the actual dismissal, including matters of which the employer was not aware but would have eventually discovered. Matters that occurred after the actual dismissal, such as a retaliatory sabotaging of the computer system or an abusive email, cannot normally be taken into account for *Polkey* reductions. An exceptional circumstance might be a conviction for assault that took place after dismissal but had nothing to do with the previous employment. If the employer can show that they would always dismiss someone in those circumstances, this may also limit compensation on the basis that the claimant would have definitely been dismissed after being convicted.

Contributory Conduct

This concept is relatively straightforward in unfair dismissal cases – if an employee has done something culpable and blameworthy that contributes to the dismissal then this can lead to a percentage reduction to both the compensatory and basic award – ***Nelson v British Broadcasting Corporation (No. 2)*** [1980] ICR 110. For example, if some aspect of a misconduct dismissal is unfair but the employee did in fact commit misconduct, thus putting himself in that situation, then his award may well be reduced for contributory fault.

In discrimination cases, the concept is less clear. It is difficult in principle to see how an individual could contribute to being discriminated against because of his age. In ***First Great Western v Waiyego*** UKEAT/0056/

18/RN, the EAT commented that a reduction for contributory fault in a discrimination case would '*rarely if ever*' arise. The EAT gave the possible example of a claim for a failure to make reasonable adjustments where the claimant is offered medical assistance unreasonably late but also does not attend the appointment. It could be argued that this would mean that she has contributed towards any loss (e.g. if her psychiatric injury became worse, or she took longer to recover as a result). However, Kerr J suggested that such an argument would be better treated as a failure to mitigate loss i.e. that the claimant should only be compensated for the time it would have taken her to recover if she had reasonably mitigated by attending the appointment. The court therefore disapproved of the previous EAT *obiter* comment in ***Way v Crouch*** [2005] ICR 1362 that contributory fault could be argued in discrimination cases.

In cases of unfair dismissal where the dismissal is also discriminatory, our view is that to avoid the ***First Great Western*** argument that contributory fault should not apply in discrimination cases, it is better for respondents to use either a *Polkey* or failure to mitigate argument as any contributory fault finding is more open to challenge.

Social security benefits

Unlike for cases of unfair dismissal, in discrimination claims, any state benefits over that period are not subject to recoupment by the Department for Work and Pensions. However, any benefits received will reduce the claimant's losses as per normal principles of tort. To do otherwise would allow the claimant a windfall.

Injury to Feelings

Compensation for age discrimination is not solely concerned with financial loss. Claimants do not have to have suffered financial loss at all to receive an award from the tribunal. Section 119(4) EqA is clear that tribunals can make injury to feelings awards even where they have not made an award under any other head of loss. It may often be the case, particularly where the age discrimination claim does not concern dismissal, that the most significant part of the remedy sought is the injury to feelings award.

When will an injury to feelings award be made?

The purpose of injury to feelings awards is to compensate the claimant for the injury they have suffered. The focus of the tribunal will be on the impact that unlawful discrimination has, in reality, had on the claimant. Discrimination will impact different people in different ways. The question is not what the impact should or could have been, but what the impact was.

The burden of proof lies with the claimant to demonstrate that they have suffered injury because of unlawful discrimination and then to prove the extent or nature of that injury. The evidence that will be required will vary from case to case. However, the EAT provided helpful guidance on such issues in ***Eddie Stobart Ltd v Graham*** [2025] EAT 14 (para.52):

- **The claimant's description of their injury**. This will usually be evidenced through the claimant's account in their witness statement of how the unlawful treatment made them feel.

- **The duration of the consequences**. The claimant should be able to explain if they have recovered and, if they have not, how long they believe the injury will continue. If the harm is continuing, the tribunal will have to consider for how long the injury might persist.

- **The effect on past, current and future work**. This should also be evidenced in the claimant's witness statement. This might include the impact on the claimant's capacity to enjoy work in the present or on the claimant's ability to look back warmly on their past experiences at work. The tribunal may also take into account how important work and career was to the claimant. This may be particularly significant in cases where claimants who have had very long service at the same company feel they have been forced out or sidelined because of their age. They may be able to contend that their job and the work that they did was a cornerstone of their life's work and identity. For long-service employees, the impact on how they view their past work and themselves is likely to be weighed heavily by the tribunal. If the respondent can adduce evidence that the claimant had previously wished to leave employment, before any discriminatory treatment, that might suggest that the impact of the discriminatory treatment was limited. However, if there is evidence to suggest that the claimant previously enjoyed their line of work and now sees it negatively or wishes to leave, then a tribunal is likely to conclude that the hurt caused is significant.

- **The effect on personal life or quality of life**. Again, this should be addressed in the claimant's witness statement. It may also be helpful to call witness evidence from a family member or another third-party who can attest to the impact on personal activities or the claimant's private life. However, it was made clear in ***Eddie Stobart*** that it will be for the tribunal, on a case-by-case basis, to determine how much weight can be given to the evidence of a family member or other similar third party. Respondents often argue that such evidence is worth little given the close relationships involved, but tribunals can find it persuasive if the witness is compelling.

Significantly, medical evidence or a diagnosis is not required for a claimant to meet the burden of proof that age discrimination has caused them harm. Injury to feelings encompasses a broad range of injury and hurt, not only injury from a medical perspective. As set out by Lord Justice Mummery in ***Vento v Chief Constable of West Yorkshire Police (No.2)*** [2003] ICR 318, CA (para.50), injury to feelings includes *'subjective feelings of upset, frustration, worry, anxiety, mental distress, fear, grief, anguish, humiliation, unhappiness, stress, depression and so on'.*

This said, whilst not mandatory, it may often be very persuasive if claimants can adduce medical evidence of any stress, anxiety or depression that they have suffered as a result of discrimination. This will particularly be the case if the respondent is alleging that the claimant is exaggerating the effect of the discrimination. Such evidence may take the form of GP or hospital records, a letter from a treating physician or therapist or even an independent medical report.

When considering the evidence that needs to be marshalled to succeed in an injury to feelings award it is important to remember that *'no tribunal will take much persuasion that the anger, distress and affront caused by the act of discrimination has injured the claimant's feelings'* (***Ministry of Defence v Cannock and ors*** [1994] ICR 918). Where the alleged injury is difficult to evidence, the nature of discrimination can be a useful guide that may assist the tribunal to infer what injury was suffered (***Eddie Stobart Ltd v Graham*** [2025] EAT 14 (para.41)).

It will in general be the case that the *'distress and humiliation suffered by the victim will be greater when the discrimination is overt, or where, even in the absence of overt signs, the victim understands the motivation at the time to be discriminatory; and in such cases the compensation will be correspondingly higher'*, as set out by the EAT in ***Taylor v XLN Telecom Ltd and others*** [2010] IRLR 499 (para.10). However, that does not mean that in principle to receive an injury to feelings award a claimant needs to have known that conduct was an act of age discrimination at the time, provided that the hurt suffered is *'still an injury attributable to the discriminatory conduct'*. In addition, unlike when calculating future financial losses, the tribunal cannot reduce a claimant's injury to feelings award because they might have been fairly dismissed in the future (***O'Donoghue v Redcar and Cleveland Borough Council*** [2001] IRLR 615, CA).

Crucially, injury to feelings awards are not punitive. I.e. their purpose is not to punish the respondent. The nature of the respondent, for example, whether they are a small or a large company with minimal or extensive resources, is therefore irrelevant. The tribunal must consider the impact on the particular claimant in front of them. They will therefore have to consider the seriousness of the discrimination and the distress caused, but also the unique vulnerabilities of the claimant.

Determining the value of the award

When considering the value of the award, tribunals should have regard to the *'value in everyday life of the sum they have in mind'* as approved by the Court of Appeal in ***Vento v Chief Constable of West Yorkshire Police (No 2)*** [2003] IRLR 102 (para.53). Awards will be determined with reference to the Vento guidelines. These can be divided into three bands.

The lower band is for *'less serious cases, such as where the act of discrimination is an isolated or one-off occurrence.'*

The middle band is for *'serious cases, which do not merit an award in the highest band.'*

The top band is for *'the most serious cases, such as where there has been a lengthy campaign of discriminatory harassment.'*

In ***Eddie Stobart Ltd v Graham*** [2025] EAT 14, the EAT provided further guidance on factors that could be considered when determining in which band an award might fall (paras.45 – 48). These can be summarised as:

- The frequency and duration of the claimant's exposure to discriminatory conduct;
- Whether the discrimination was 'overt';
- The existence of ridicule or exposure and whether discrimination takes place in front of others may increase the harm caused;
- Whether the discrimination reflects or exposes an asymmetry of power, influence and information.

The above is not an exhaustive list. There are many other factors that a tribunal might take into account when determining the size of the injury to feelings award. Some of those factors that come up in practice, together with examples, are:

- Whether discrimination has been suffered at the hands of one individual or at the hands of a number of colleagues (***Giwa-Amu v Department of Work and Pensions*** [2020] 2 WLUK 454 (para.88)).

- Whether the claimant has suffered past trauma or previous similar discrimination. For example, if a claimant has experienced age discrimination in previous employment, that may mean that the impact of subsequent discriminatory conduct is greater and more hurtful.

- Whether the claimant is highly vulnerable or has pre-existing mental health issues.

- If the job in question was casual or part-time, it may lead a tribunal in some circumstances to conclude that the harm was lesser (***Orlando v Didcot Power Station Sports and Social Club*** [1996] IRLR 262, EAT).

- Whether the claimant has participated in the banter themselves or made comments about their own age. An example of this, as referred to in Chapter 5 on Harassment related to age, is the case of ***Crompton v Eden Private Staff Ltd*** ET Case No. 1404549/19. In ***Crompton***, the award for injury to feelings was in the lower band. Part of the reasoning for this was that the claimant had described herself as having a *'senior moment'* after making a mistake at work.

The financial range of each band is updated annually from 6 April in the form of Presidential Guidance to reflect inflation. The current ranges provided, which are in force from 5 April 2025, are as follows:

Lower band: £1,200 – £12,100

Middle band: £12,100 – £36,400

Upper band: £36,400 – £60,700

There is nothing that says that awards must fall within the Vento bands. There is no upper limit in principle on injury to feelings awards. Moreover, in ***HM Prison Service v Johnson*** UKEAT/1033/95, as approved in ***Vento***, the EAT was clear that awards should not be so low as to diminish respect for the law. This said, in ***Vento***, it was also held that an award should be greater than the upper limit of the top band only *'in the most exceptional case'*. Awards will therefore almost always fall within the Vento bands. An injury to feelings award that falls outside of the Vento bands may in fact be open to challenge.

Where different forms of discrimination based on different protected characteristics arise out of different factual discriminatory acts, the tribunal should assess the injury to feelings caused by those acts separately. The tribunal can then look at the total figure and ensure that it remains proportionate. However, if discrimination on the basis of different protected characteristics arises from the same index discriminatory acts, the tribunal should determine the impact on a claimant as a whole, instead of looking at each form of discrimination in isolation (***Al Jumard v Clwyd Leisure Ltd and others*** [2008] IRLR 345 EAT (para.48)).

The tribunal does not have to make an award in the band suggested by the claimant in their schedule of loss. It is open to a tribunal to find that the proposed injury to feelings award and Vento band is too small a sum for the injury caused. However, it is rare that a tribunal will make an award higher than that proposed by the claimant. Thought should therefore be given when preparing the schedule of loss and submissions on remedy as to which band is appropriate, for example by considering the case law. An exaggerated figure is unlikely to assist a claimant's case.

It should be noted that the well-known *'thin skull'* rule applies to discrimination cases too. If an individual has a much higher level of injury to feelings than the average person would have from the same act of discrimination, this is not a reason to reduce an award. The discriminator takes the victim as they find them.

Age discrimination awards

Every case will be looked at on its specific facts. However, looking at comparable cases and the award given in those cases will assist when making submissions to the tribunal on the most appropriate band. Just as in personal injury cases, it is appropriate to use an inflation calculator to estimate the value of the precedent case award at the time of the remedy decision in the new case. The uplift for a precedent that is only a few years old can be surprisingly high, as the examples below show. This is because the Vento bands have increased significantly, in line with inflation, since 2017. Below are examples of three age discrimination claims, each of which fell within a different band.

Giwa-Amu v Department of Work and Pensions [2020] 2 WLUK 454 is an example of an age discrimination case where an award was made in the top band. The claimant also brought claims of race discrimination, sex discrimination and victimisation. The tribunal considered whether it was possible to separate the injury to feelings caused by each act of discrimination and concluded that it would be artificial to do so. The award given was therefore a global award for all the identified acts of discrimination. The claimant was an administrative officer who was 55 years old at the time of her training and brought claims concerning discriminatory bullying that she said she had experienced at the hands of various other trainees. The claimant alleged that, in part, this bullying was age discrimination and that she was targeted, publicly ridiculed and left out because of her age. The tribunal took into account that the claimant was distressed by a number of people's discriminatory actions, which led her to feel ostracised from the group and betrayed. They also considered the fact that the claimant alleged that the injury she suffered was ongoing at the time of the remedy hearing. Taking that into account, the tribunal made an award at the lower end of the top Vento band of £27,500 for injury to feelings and £7,500 for aggravated damages. In May 2025, this award would be worth approximately £37,000 for injury to feelings and £10,000 for aggravated damages.

Portelli v London Legal + Imaging Solutions Limited ET Case Nos. 220187/2018 & 2205855/2018 is an example of an age discrimination case where an award was made in the middle band. The claimant worked for a company that provided printing services to law firms. The claimant had been employed for 17 years. In April 2018, he was dismissed. The claimant alleged that he had been dismissed because he was older and therefore more expensive than the people who replaced him, and that this was direct age discrimination. The tribunal upheld the claim of age discrimination and made an award for injury to feelings in the middle Vento band. The tribunal found that the claimant was distressed by the dismissal and that the experience and the loss of valuable employment had caused him anxiety. They further held that it was significant that the respondent had *'failed to articulate adequately or at all the reason for this dismissal and that this added to his distress'* (para.131). Furthermore, while it was acknowledged that only a single act of discrimination had been found, namely the dismissal, the tribunal made clear that *'not all single acts of discrimination are equal'* (para.134). It was added that a *'single act which is the end of the course of conduct may well be seen as more damaging and more serious than something which is truly an isolated incident'* (para.139). The tribunal therefore made an award in the higher part of the middle Vento band of £22,500, £29,500 in May 2025

Irving v TUI Airways Ltd ET Case No.4101640/2022 is an example of an age discrimination case where an award was made in the lower band. In *Irving*, the claimant, who was 42 and had worked for TUI Airways for 20 years, was dismissed by reason of redundancy. Length of service was the sole selection criterion for the claimant's redundancy. It was alleged that this amounted to age discrimination. The claimant could not possibly have had more than 25 years' service because of her age. The staff who were retained under the selection criteria had over 25 years' service. The tribunal upheld that this was indirect age discrimination. The award for injury to feelings was, however, in the lower band. The tribunal took into account the fact that the discrimination was a one-off process. The tribunal found that there was no evidence that the redundancy process was deliberately discriminatory or that there was *'unpleasantness'* relating to the issue. For this reason, the award was made of £6,000 in the middle of the lower Vento band. This is equivalent to £6,650 in May 2025.

Other potentially helpful precedents referenced elsewhere in this book are:

Crompton v Eden Private Staff Ltd ET Case No. 1404549/19 – injury to feelings of £900 (£1,200 in May 2025). Alleged banter about Alzheimer's made to the claimant was harassment, but no complaint was made at the time and the claimant herself had mentioned her own *'senior moment'*.

Cubbin v Age UK ET Case No. 2210200/2023 – injury to feelings of £4,000 (£4,100 in May 2025). The claimant was subject to harassment when he applied for a job and was given feedback which said his ability was not reflective of his 40 years' experience thereby imposing a higher standard upon Mr Cubbin than the *'must have'* for the role.

A v Bonmarche Ltd ET Case No.4107766/19 – injury to feelings of £18,000 (£24,000 in May 2025). The claimant was harassed by her manager particularly related to being a menopausal woman. She resigned as a result.

Jolly v Royal Berkshire NHS Foundation Trust ET Case No. 3324869/2017 – injury to feelings of £20,000 (£27,000 in May 2025). The 86 year-old claimant was harassed and dismissed due to her age and disability. The respondent undertook a capability process tainted by discriminatory and distressing assumptions about frailty and being *'stuck in old secretarial ways'*.

Ewart v The Chancellor, Masters and Scholars of the University of Oxford ET Case No. 3324911/2017 – injury to feelings of £22,500 (£30,000 in May 2025). The claimant was subject to indirect age discrimination in the form of mandatory retirement which was not justified.

Matar v Imperial College Healthcare NHS Trust ET Case No. 2206291/2018 – injury to feelings of £25,000 and aggravated damages of £5,000 (£31,000 and £6,000 in May 2025). The older claimant was not offered training and retirement was discussed with him, whereas a younger comparator was offered training. Various acts of age discrimination contributed to his constructive dismissal.

In our experience, if a tribunal finds that employment has been terminated due to discrimination, a lower band award will almost never be appropriate. Equally, awards in the upper band are very rare. This means that in practice, the vast majority of awards involving dismissal will be in the middle band and are often in the lower half of that middle band.

Aggravated Damages

Aggravated damages are intended to compensate a claimant for further distress caused by aggravating features of the unlawful discrimination. An aggravating feature will be where the respondent has acted in a *'high-handed, malicious, insulting or oppressive manner in committing the act of discrimination'* (***Alexander v Home Office*** [1988] ICR 685, CA). This can be broken down into three potentially aggravating features set out in ***Commissioner of Police of the Metropolis v Shaw*** [2012] ICR 464, EAT (para.22):

- Where the manner in which the wrong was committed was particularly upsetting. This may be any exceptional conduct which has the effect of seriously increasing the claimant's distress.
- Where there was a discriminatory motive. The claimant must have been aware of the discriminatory motive.
- Where later conduct, usually the respondent's conduct when defending tribunal proceedings, increases the injury suffered. This might also, in some situations, include a failure or refusal to apologise.

Just as with injury to feelings awards, aggravated damages are not punitive. They are intended to compensate the claimant for further harm that they have suffered. Therefore, the claimant must demonstrate that there is a causal link between the aggravating factor and any further injury or distress that they experienced.

There has been some uncertainty in the case law as to whether aggravated damages awards should be made separate from the injury to feelings award, or whether they should be included as part of the injury to feelings award. The EAT has suggested that aggravated damages are a subset of the broader injury to feelings award. Care should be taken not to award the claimant for the same injury twice, once through aggravated damages and once through an injury to feelings award (***Commissioner of Police of the Metropolis v Shaw*** [2012] ICR 464, EAT (para.23)). If a claimant is seeking an aggravated damages award, they must therefore be prepared to explain why the harm for which aggravated damages should be awarded is separate from the harm which has been compensated for in any separate award for injury to feelings. When considering the size of any award for aggravated damages, the tribunal will keep in mind what is proportionate, considering any injury to feelings award that has already been made. As above, awards were made for aggravated damages together with injury to feelings in the cases of ***Giwa-Amu*** and ***Matar.*** It should be noted that awards for aggravated damages are rare.

Exemplary Damages

Unlike aggravated damages and indeed all the other heads of claim described above, exemplary damages are intended to punish the discriminator. They are the most exceptional of all awards and, in tribunal, will only be made in cases of oppressive, arbitrary or unconstitutional acts by government departments or where the employer's discriminatory conduct results in a profit which may exceed the claimant's compensation – ***Rookes v Barnard and ors*** [1964] AC 1129, HL. The threshold for establishing such behaviour is high – ***Ministry of Defence v Fletcher*** [2010] IRLR 25, EAT.

Personal Injury

In addition to claiming injury to feelings, in some cases claimants will wish to claim damages for injury that is medically provable. In age discrimination cases, this will likely be psychiatric injury as opposed to any other physical injury.

The claimant does not have to prove that any injury they have suffered was reasonably foreseeable to their employer. However, they must prove that there is a causal link between any injury suffered and the unlawful discrimination experienced. This will often be a challenge as it may be difficult to show what caused a psychiatric injury, particularly where there are multiple contributing possible causes.

If a claimant is seeking an award for personal injury, they will likely need to obtain medical evidence, usually this will be in the form of a report from a treating psychiatrist or an independent medical expert. Medical evidence will be particularly important where there is a dispute over the cause of any injury. Although it is always advisable to obtain a medical report to support a claim for personal injury damages, the EAT have made clear that it is not necessary in every case, even where the personal injury claim is not low value – ***Hampshire County Council v Wyatt*** EAT 0013/16.

An assessment of damages for personal injury should consider the claimant's pre-existing conditions and vulnerabilities, both whether they have been a cause of the injury itself and where they might, in the future, have led to a similar injury if the unlawful discrimination had not happened. An award for personal injury may therefore be reduced by the tribunal to reflect the fact that the injury might have occurred in the future, even if the discrimination had not taken place.

If the evidence suggests that a pre-existing condition or other event was itself a cause of the psychiatric injury, this may also impact the award to which the claimant will be entitled. Guidance on the approach to situations where a claimant suffers psychiatric injury as a result of multiple causes was set out by Lady Hale in ***Hatton v Sutherland and other cases*** [2002] ICR 613, CA. It was made clear that the employer should be liable for the harm that is attributable to the unlawful discrimination. The employer should not have to compensate the claimant for the entire injury if there were other causes of the claimant's condition unless the harm is truly indivisible. However, it is for the employer to raise the issue of apportionment if they think such an issue is relevant.

Damages for personal injury are awarded under the heads of 'general damages' for pain, suffering or loss of amenity and 'special damages' for financial loss that flows from the injury.

General damages will be awarded with reference to the Judicial College Guidelines (previously the Judicial Studies Board / JSB Guidelines), which set out the appropriate level of award for different extents of psychiatric injury and post-traumatic stress disorder. Further detail on the Judicial College Guidelines, now in its 17th edition published in April 2024, is outside of the scope of this book and is not dealt with further here.

Special damages may be awarded where the injury is so severe that the claimant is unable to work. In age discrimination cases, seeking special damages may be more common as claimants who suffer psychiatric injury towards the end of their working life may not have sufficient time to recover and rejoin the workforce. If the claimant is rendered unable to work again and will suffer life-long loss, the approach that the tribunal will take will be the same as the conventional approach in personal injury cases. This will be to use the Ogden Tables to provide a multiplier which will then be multiplied by a multiplicand (the claimant's annual net loss) – see section on career loss above. If the claimant is rendered unable to work for a shorter period, the normal approach to loss of earnings taken in discriminatory dismissals, as described earlier in this chapter, will be used.

When considering both general and special damages, tribunals will keep in mind the risk of double recovery. If an award has already been made for loss of earnings and injury to feelings, it may be that there is considerable crossover with any award that might be made for personal injury. When seeking an award for personal injury, it is therefore important to give thought to why the personal injury suffered is separable from any asserted injury to feelings.

While it is outside the scope of this book, it is also noted that claims for personal injury occurring at work can also be pursued outside of the employment tribunal and through the civil courts.

Accelerated receipt

In cases where future loss is significant (i.e. more than a year of future losses), the tribunal should consider imposing a reduction on the future loss element to reflect the fact that the claimant could invest the lump sum award, earn interest and end up receiving more than she would have received had she been earning her salary. This is known as a reduction for accelerated receipt. ***Bentwood Bros (Manchester) Ltd v Shepherd*** [2003] EWCA Civ 380 is an example of such a case. The Ogden tables (available online) can assist with an appropriate multiplier which will depend on how far the future losses extend and also on the current discount rate under the Damages Act 1996. As of January 2025, this was

+0.5%. Respondents should remember to suggest such a discount to the tribunal in order to minimise any award.

ACAS Uplift

The ACAS Code of Practice 1 on Disciplinary and Grievance Procedures (2015) provides guidance that should be followed by both employers and employees when going through a disciplinary process or when a grievance has been raised. It can also apply to performance dismissals but not to most other procedures, such as ill-health or redundancy. If either employer or employee unreasonably fails to follow the code, a tribunal can award an uplift or make a deduction of up to 25% of compensation if it is just and equitable to do so (s207A Trade Union and Labour Relations (Consolidation) Act 1992). This discretion applies to a number of types of awards including discrimination claims under the Equality Act 2010.

There is little guidance as to which percentage the tribunal should select. It would make sense that a complete failure to adopt any procedure could lead to a 25% uplift. However, the tribunal must take into account the actual financial level of the award as this could be significant (***Acetrip Ltd v Dogra*** UKEAT/0238/18/BA). In this case, the EAT noted the guidance in ***Wardle v Credit Agricole Corporate and Investment Bank*** [2011] ICR 1290 applies to the current ACAS provisions. The Court of Appeal also found that an uplift to the maximum level should be very rare indeed (albeit we note that at the time of the ***Wardle*** decision this was 50%).

Interest

The tribunal can award interest in the calculation of compensation by means of the Employment Tribunals (Interest on Awards in Discrimination Cases) Regulations 1996 (S.I. 1996/2803). This sets awards for discrimination apart from other awards made by the tribunal, which normally do not accrue interest except for the interest that applies to all unpaid judgments.

A claimant does not have to apply for interest or set it out in their schedule of loss. A tribunal is required to consider whether they should award interest regardless of whether the claimant raises the point (Reg 2(1)). The parties can agree on the amount of interest to be awarded, and often it will be easy to do so. However, if the parties cannot agree, the tribunal will award interest based on the rules set out in Reg 3. The tribunal will set out in their written reasons the interest awarded and, if the sum was not agreed by the parties, how that interest has been calculated (Reg 7(1)). The tribunal will have to provide their reasons if they decide not to award interest at all (Reg 7(2)).

Interest on a discrimination claim is calculated at the rate prescribed under Reg 3(2), which is currently 8 per cent. The regulations apply simple interest. This will be the same for interest on any award for unlawful discrimination. However, the date from which the interest is calculated will be different depending on whether the award is for injury to feelings or whether it falls under any other head of loss. It is important to note that while the regulations set out the approach detailed below, if there would be '*serious injustice*' caused by that approach, then the tribunal can deviate from the regulations and calculate interest for different periods (Reg 6(3)).

When calculating interest for injury to feelings awards, interest will be calculated from the date of the act of the discrimination complained of and will end on the day that the tribunal calculates the interest (Reg 6(1)(a)).

In some cases, it will not be obvious on what date the act of discrimination started. In cases where it is found that there has been discrimination that is a course of continuing conduct, parties may not agree on how interest should be calculated. Practitioners should therefore be prepared to make submissions on when they say the discriminatory act began.

When calculating interest for other losses that occur over a period such as earnings, interest will be calculated from the '*mid-point date*' and will end on the day that the tribunal calculates the interest (Reg 6(1)(b)). As set out in Reg 4(2), the mid-point date is the day halfway between the date of the discrimination and the date of calculation. Interest will not be awarded for losses arising after the date of calculation.

Tax and Grossing Up

The general rule in discrimination cases is that successful claimants will have to pay tax on awards of compensation. The major exceptions are that the first £30,000 is usually tax-free and that awards of injury to feelings attributable to acts before dismissal are not subject to tax. This means that it may be necessary to ask the tribunal to split an injury to feelings award into compensation for conduct occurring before dismissal and compensation as a result of the dismissal so that tax is easier to calculate.

Because compensation is taxable, tribunals should gross up any compensation such that claimants receive the correct amount of compensation in their pockets, after being taxed. The amount of grossing up will be different depending on the tax bands applicable for each individual claimant.

For example, as of 2025, a claimant who has already received over £125,140 in other income in the tax year when the award is made will have to pay 45% income tax on the entirety of the award. If that award is £130,000, then first the £30,000 tax free sum is subtracted. The grossing up calculation is then (£100,000/0.55) = £181,818. The £30,000 tax-free element is then added back in, such that the tribunal will have to award (£181,818 + £30,000) = £211,818, in order that the claimant is left with £130,000 after tax. A common mistake is to use a calculation of £100,000 x 0.45 to calculate the tax by which £100,000 should be grossed up. This is incorrect and will result in the claimant being significantly undercompensated.

For 20% tax, the net sum must be divided by 0.8 to get the gross figure. For 40% tax, the figure is 0.6. For 45% tax, the figure is 0.55.

When the claimant has no or modest other income, it is necessary to do a series of calculations to take into account multiple tax bands. For example, for an award (made in 2025 in England or Wales, not Scotland) of £100,000 where there is no other income:

- **Start with the net award.** This is the award the tribunal wishes to make after all adjustments of compensation have been taken into account. Here, the net award is £100,000.

- **Subtract the £30,000 tax-free allowance from the net award to get a net sum to be grossed up (A).** A is £70,000 after deduction of the tax-free £30,000.

- **Note any personal allowance (B).** £12,570 is the standard personal allowance for those with income less than £100,000. It is subject to nil rate tax.

- **Work out the gross figure for the basic tax band (C).** In this case, this is the entirety of the basic tax band as published by HMRC, i.e. £37,770. Basic tax rate applies at 20% to this band.

- **Work out the net figure for the basic tax band (D).** To calculate the net figure for that basic 20% band, the calculation is £37,770 x 0.8 = £30,216.

- **Add the personal allowance (B) to the gross figure for the basic tax band (C) to get a running gross total (E).** The running gross total is (£12,570 + £37,770) = £50,340.

- **Add the personal allowance (B) to the net figure for the basic tax band (D) to get a running net total (F).** Adding the personal allowance back in provides a running net total of (£12,570 + £30,216) = £42,786.

- **Subtract the running net total (F) from the net sum to be grossed up (A) to get a remaining net figure for grossing up (G).** The remaining net amount of the award is (£70,000 – £42,786) = £27,214. This must also be grossed up.

- **Gross up the remaining net figure (G) to get the grossed up higher rate figure (H).** The remaining £27,214 will all fall into the higher tax band of 40%. Therefore it must be grossed up by dividing by 0.6. (£27,214/0.6) = £45,357.

- **Add together the running gross total (E) with the grossed up higher rate figure (G) to get a gross taxable figure (I).** The grossed-up figure based on the original £70,000 is therefore (£50,340 + £45,357) = £95,697.

- **Add the gross taxable figure (I) to the £30,000 tax free allowance to calculate the grand total.** The tax-free £30,000 that was deducted at the start needs to be added back in: (£95,697 + £30,000) = £125,697.

The tribunal will therefore order a gross payment of £125,697 of which the claimant is likely to pay around £25,697 tax.

The use of an online salary calculator can assist in checking the approximate correct figure. It should be noted that salary calculator figures may include payment of national insurance which is not part of the above grossing up calculation. It appears that as HMRC do not recoup employee national insurance contributions from tribunal awards, there is no need to take them into account when grossing up. This, together with other complexities such as the gradual loss of personal allowance above £100,000 show why, on large awards, accountancy or tax advice may be necessary. Lump sum pension contributions and gift aid may also complicate calculations.

Crucially, a claimant should not forget to raise the issue of grossing up at tribunal. It is easily overlooked and, as illustrated, could result in a huge loss to the claimant.

Order of Adjustments

In discrimination cases, financial losses are calculated in the following order:

1. Calculate the claimant's financial loss taking into account when the claimant did or should have got a new job. This will include any predicted future losses.

2. Deduct any relevant amounts received from the respondent, such as pay in lieu of notice.

3. Reduce by any sums actually earned in mitigation.

4. Make any *Polkey*-style reduction on the basis the claimant's employment would have ended anyway.

5. Decrease for accelerated receipt of compensation in respect of future loss.

6. Apply any uplift/reduction regarding the ACAS code.

7. Add interest.

8. Gross up.

CHAPTER TEN

HOW TO BRING AN AGE DISCRIMINATION CLAIM

- *Who can claim for age discrimination at work?*
- *Against whom?*
- *How to claim*
- *Time limits and extensions*
- *How to defend*
- *Further Information*
- *Preliminary hearings (closed and open)*
- *List of issues*
- *Evidence*
- *Full Hearings in ETs*
- *Appeals*

This chapter contains practical advice for parties making or facing age discrimination claims and navigating the employment tribunal ("ET") system. Many books could be devoted to the subject of the practice and procedure in the ET system, so this chapter is necessarily brief and in summary form. There are hopefully useful precedents included in the appendices to this chapter.

The ET has exclusive jurisdiction over allegations of discrimination in employment – s.120 of the Equality Act 2010 ('EqA'). The Employment Tribunal Procedure Rules 2024 (2024 UK SI No. 1155) are applicable to all ET processes ("the ET Rules"):

https://www.legislation.gov.uk/uksi/2024/1155/contents/made

Claims for age discrimination can only be brought in the civil jurisdiction (county courts or High Court) where they are outside an employment relationship (e.g. in relation to the provision of services or public functions, etc.). The Civil Procedure Rules apply to such claims and are outside the scope of this book.

Who can claim for age discrimination at work?

The EqA gives protection to a wider category of workers than does the Employment Rights Act 1996, so more people are eligible to claim discrimination than could claim unfair dismissal. Employment under the EqA includes employees and apprentices but also contractors who are personally engaged to do work (s.83(2) EqA). That means that, although truly self-employed contractors who work on their own account, especially those working through their own limited company, for example, are not covered by the EqA, most other workers are covered (see the Supreme Court's opinion in ***Uber BV v Aslam*** [2021] UKSC 5, [2021] IRLR 407).

Workers can claim not only for discrimination which occurred at work (ss.39-40 EqA), but also for discriminatory acts/harassment arising out of or closely connected to an employment relationship which used to exist (within the meaning of the EqA) – s.108 EqA. A common claim in this regard is in relation to discriminatory references from former employers, which are caught by s.108 EqA so are actionable in the ET.

Applicants for work can also claim age discrimination (under ss.39-40 EqA) if the arrangements made for deciding to whom to offer employment amount to discrimination.

In the context of work, the EqA protection also covers (among others):

- contract workers (under s.41 EqA) which includes agency workers, temporary workers supplied by a temping agency, and workers employed by a concessionaire to work in a department store;

- partners and members of limited liability partnerships (under ss.44 and 45 EqA respectively);

- Barristers, advocates and office holders (under ss.47 – 51 EqA);

- People using employment agencies (under s.55 EqA);

- Trade union members or applicants for trade union membership (s.57 EqA).

Against whom can a worker claim for age discrimination at work?

In broad terms, a worker can claim against an employer, a fellow employee, a recruitment agency or certain third parties.

An employer could be any legal entity, like a limited company, a public body, a partnership or an individual. This is the other party to the contract governing the work. Usually, it is the party named in the contract of employment or equivalent document, unless there has been an error or a transfer of employment (under the Transfer of Undertakings (Protection of Employment) Regulations 2006).

The employer is vicariously liable for the actions for its employees and agents in the course of their employment (under s.109 EqA and see ***CLFIS (UK) Ltd v Reynolds*** [2015] IRLR 562). There is a statutory defence, under s.109(4) which is available where the employer can show that it took all reasonable steps to prevent the discriminator from doing the thing complained of or anything of that description, but this is, in practice, very difficult to demonstrate – ***Allay (UK) Ltd v Gehlen***

UKEAT/0031/20, 4th February 2021, unreported. Where an employer pleads the statutory defence under s.109(4) EqA, the focus of the tribunal is often on what the employer did before the discriminatory act to prevent discrimination, rather than only on what the employer did in response to the discrimination. An employer cannot be liable for the age discriminatory actions of third parties against their employees (unless the employer's reason for not intervening in the discriminatory acts of third parties is discriminatory in itself). There are proposals contained in the Employment Rights Bill 2024 to introduce employer liability for third-party harassment where an employer fails to take "all reasonable steps" to prevent such harassment. These proposals are, at the time of writing, still in the consultation stage but it is likely this will come into force in or around October 2026. Practitioners are advised to keep an eye on the progress of the Bill.

In most cases, the claimant will only name their employer as the respondent – that is because usually (a) they have the deepest pockets, and (b) they are the party most likely to be liable. It is also permissible for a worker to name an individual colleague, perhaps a manager, who was personally responsible for the discrimination, as a respondent. This colleague must either be an employee or a worker of the same employer, or an agent of the employer who committed discriminatory acts while acting on the employer's behalf. A colleague of a claimant who was in fact a self-employed consultant cannot be liable under the EqA. An individual employee or agent will only be liable under the EqA (s.110 EqA) if the discriminatory act was done in the course of their employment, or by an agent with the principal's authority. There is a defence available to individual respondents under s.110(3) EqA where they reasonably relied upon a statement of the employer to the effect that the thing they subsequently did would not be a contravention of EqA 2010.

A claimant who successfully claims against a fellow employee or agent can recover the same remedy against the person found personally liable, as would be available against an employer (see Chapter 9 Remedies). Nevertheless it would be wise to name both the employer and an individual respondent, rather than only to name an individual as a respondent.

An employer, principal, employee or agent may also be liable for instructing, causing or inducing contraventions of the EqA, or for aiding contraventions of EqA, under ss.111, 112 EqA respectively (see ***Bailey v Stonewall Equality Ltd*** [2024] EAT 119).

How to claim in the ET

A person who feels they have been the victim of age discrimination in the context of their work, in circumstances where liability arises under the EqA, needs to act quickly to enforce their rights. It is more important to present a claim form in time than it is to gather all the information needed on every aspect of the claim before issuing. County courts and the High Court do deal with some employment claims (such as breach of contract or claims for injunctions), but employment tribunals have the exclusive jurisdiction for employment-related discrimination claims.

ACAS EC

The first step is to contact ACAS to participate in the obligatory ACAS Early Conciliation ("ACAS EC") process. There is an on-line form available at www.acas.org.uk/early-conciliation.

In the vast majority of cases, and in any case where age discrimination is being claimed, the claim will be rejected unless the ACAS EC process has been completed before the claim is presented to the ET. It is a very simple process, which has as its aim settlement of the claims by agreement, before the ET is involved.

It is very important that this is done within 3 months of the act complained of (see detailed rules on time limits and possible extensions below). Participation in ACAS EC does not cost either party any money, is confidential (so it will not be revealed to any judge dealing with the matter subsequently) and it is frequently the case that litigants could achieve different, and perhaps more desirable, outcomes from a conciliation process than they would ultimately achieve in the slow, expensive and stressful ET system.

It is important for both parties to think about a realistic settlement which could be offered, which would avoid the issuing of a claim. Chapter 9 Remedies should be helpful to anticipate, if possible, what an ET might award, if the claimant were to succeed at a full hearing (which could easily be 2-3 years from the date of the discrimination happening). It is important to quantify likely costs, especially if there is an intention to instruct lawyers, because it is very rare for costs to be recovered by the winning party from the losing party in an ET. Sometimes it is worth being creative – would an apology or a plan of action (particularly if employment continues) assist the parties to move forward without litigation? Could an agreed reference assist the parties to reach agreement on settlement? The parties should both approach ACAS EC with an open mind, and an objective to avoid the stress, inconvenience, cost and risk of litigation, if reasonably possible.

The ET time limit is put on hold for the duration of ACAS EC (which is usually up to 6 weeks). A settlement reached during ACAS EC is legally binding and, once reached and finalised, means that the parties cannot pursue an action in the ET. If a settlement is not reached during ACAS EC, there is nothing to prevent the parties from settling the action after that point.

Time limits/extensions of time

Age discrimination claims must be presented to the ET within 3 months of the discrimination happening, according to s.123 EqA. Putting aside the effect of ACAS EC, this means that if a claimant alleges that the decision on 15th April 2025 not to promote her was discriminatory on the grounds of age, the claimant will have until 14th July 2025 to present the claim.

Now that ACAS EC is an obligatory process before the claim is issued, the time limits have been altered to enable the parties to undertake that process (s.140B EqA). If the claimant contacts ACAS in the first two months after the act complained of, the period of ACAS EC (that is, the time between the date ACAS was contacted, and the date ACAS issued the certificate) is not counted in the 3-month time limit. If the claimant contacts ACAS in the third month (more than two months after the act complained of but within 3 months) the claimant will benefit from an extension of the limitation period as the claimant will be given an extra month from the date of the ACAS certificate before a claim has to be submitted. This means that a claimant always has at least a month after the end of ACAS EC to present a claim.

If in doubt, it is best to ensure that ACAS is contacted within three months (count three months minus one day from the act complained of) and to present the claim form within a month of obtaining the ACAS EC certificate.

In most cases, the claimant is complaining of more than one act of discrimination. Ideally, the claim form should be presented within three months of all the acts. Where discriminatory conduct continues over a period, the statute allows the time limit to start running from the end of that period (see ***Barclays Bank plc v Kapur and ors*** [1991] ICR 208, HL, ***Aziz v FDA*** [2010] EWCA Civ 304, CA). There is no requirement that the discriminatory conduct must relate to the same protected characteristic over the period (***Worcestershire Health and Care NHS Trust v Allen*** [2024] EAT 40 the EAT).

For example, a manager teases a younger employee about his "babyface" every day for four months, and then promotes an older colleague, with less experience than the younger colleague, on the basis the older colleague's grey hair gives him more gravitas and credibility. As long as the claim is presented within three months (not counting the ACAS EC) of the last time the manager referred to "babyface" and within three months of the promotion, the claim will probably be in time.

Sometimes the discrimination complained of is about a failure to do something, rather than a positive action. In this case, time starts to run from the date the purported discriminator made the decision not to act. If a claimant who is over 50 years old suggests that he has been passed over for promotion, in favour of a candidate who was significantly younger than him, time starts to run from the time the respondent decided not to promote the claimant.

It is not always easy to identify the date on which a decision not to do something was made. The EqA, at s.123(4), states that in the absence of evidence to the contrary, a person (P) is to be taken to decide on failure to do something (a) when P does an act inconsistent with doing it, or (b) if P does no inconsistent act, on the expiry of the period in which P might reasonably have been expected to do it. In some cases, there will be positive evidence that the decision happened on a particular date. However, usually, an omission is deemed to have taken place "*when the period expires within which he might reasonably have been expected to do the failed act if it was to be done*" (***Blackbay Ventures Ltd t/a Chemistree v Gahir*** [2014] ICR 747 EAT (para.99)).

Tribunals can be persuaded to extend time to enable a claim, which was presented outside the 3-month time limit, to proceed, if the ET considers that it is just and equitable to do so (see s.123(1)(b) EqA). The Court of Appeal in ***Abertawe Bro Morgannwg University Local Health Board v Morgan*** [2018] ICR 1194, described the breadth of discretion to extend time to present discrimination claims as "*wide*" (and see ***Jones v Secretary of State for Health and Social Care*** [2024] EAT 2). Whether the ET determines this point at an open preliminary hearing or a full hearing, it is important for the claimant to provide evidence on why the claim was presented late, and why it is just and equitable to extend time. This should include reference to the balance of prejudice between the parties (i.e. how much the parties are disadvantaged by the application to extend being granted or refused); and the merits of the claims – see ***Adedeji v University Hospitals Birmingham NHS Foundation Trust*** [2021] ICR D5, CA, ***Kumari v Greater Manchester Mental Health NHS Foundation Trust*** [2022] EAT 132.

The claim form (ET1)

The only way the parties can issue a claim in the ET is to use the form called an ET1. This can be downloaded from:

https://assets.publishing.service.gov.uk/media/65bcbd214a666f000d1747ba/ET1_0224.pdf

In broad terms, the ET1 form requires the claimant to give:

- Details of the parties (including all respondents, if more than one);
- The ACAS EC number;
- Employment details (including dates and earnings);
- Ticks in boxes to indicate what claims are being presented;
- The background and details of the claims (often presented in a separate document filed with the ET1, known as the Particulars of Claim);
- A summary of the compensation or remedy sought;
- Details of any representative.

The claim form can be submitted online, without any fee being payable, at:

https://www.claim-employment-tribunals.service.gov.uk/

The particulars of claim

It is important to include every legal claim to be pursued in the ET1 form because claims may not be permitted to be included later. All the detail might not be known at this early stage but the essential elements of the claim (both factual and legal) should be included in the clearest way possible for the tribunal to understand. This book is designed to assist with focus on the main elements of the claim, by the inclusion of bullet points at the beginning of every chapter dealing with a particular type of discrimination. The claimant should tell the ET in writing what they are complaining about and how it is alleged it constitutes age discrimination. Section 8 of the ET1 should be completed with the details of the claim, but if more space is required, it is often the case that a separate document called "Particulars of Claim" is attached to the ET1.

In ***Hendricks v Commissioner of Police for the Metropolis*** [2003] ICR 530, Lord Justice Mummery in the Court of Appeal urged parties and tribunals "*to keep the discrimination proceedings within reasonable bounds by concentrating on the most serious and the more recent allegations*".

An example of a simple Particulars of Claim in a fictional age discrimination case is attached at Appendix 1. Note the legal heading, which is not obligatory but useful.

Duplication of or overlap between direct discrimination and harassment claims

It is often the case that the same factual scenario can amount to both direct age discrimination and harassment related to age (see Chapter 5 Harassment and Chapter 2 Direct age discrimination). For example, where an employer, because she believes that younger staff are more attractive to her clientele, decides to base all younger employees at the front-of-house of a restaurant, and keep all older employees in behind-the-scenes roles which involve less pleasant working conditions ("the Restaurant Example"), this is arguably both direct discrimination and harassment. There is less favourable treatment of the older employees because of age, and an employee could also allege that this was unwanted conduct related to age which had the effect of creating a degrading, humiliating or offensive environment. The conduct needing to be "*related to age*" for harassment claims is a looser connection to age than causation as is required by s.13 EqA for direct discrimination, so it might be that harassment is more likely to succeed. It is possible, though, that the treatment is less favourable but does not create an intimidating, hostile, degrading, humiliating or offensive environment for the claimant or violate their dignity, in which case, a claim of direct age discrimination is more appropriate. Claimants ought to bear in mind that direct age discrimination can also be legally justified if the respondent shows that the treatment is a proportionate means of achieving a legitimate aim, but harassment cannot be justified, legally.

It is usually better to choose which claim is more likely to succeed and plead (meaning, include in the claim form) the case only characterised in that way, but if there is doubt as to which is more likely to succeed, both claims can be pleaded "*further or in the alternative*".

A tribunal will consider all allegations pleaded as both direct age discrimination and age-related harassment as allegations of harassment first. If any specific factual allegation is not proven, it can be dismissed as an allegation of both harassment and direct discrimination. If the factual allegation is proven, then the tribunal will apply the statutory test for harassment under s.26 EqA. If that allegation of harassment is made out, then it will be dismissed as an allegation of direct discrimination because under s.212(1) EqA the definition of detriment does not include conduct which amounts to harassment. If the factual allegation is proven, but the statutory test for harassment is not made out, the tribunal will then consider whether the allegation amounts to direct discrimination under s.13 EqA. The tribunal will not uphold both claims of direct discrimination and harassment.

Overlap of claims more generally

In any event, it is a good discipline not to plead every factual circumstance which might, even if rather tenuously, constitute different forms of discrimination, as every form of discrimination. In the Restaurant Example, as above, it might theoretically be possible to argue that there was a practice of having the stereotypically attractive employees front-of-house, and the older employees were less likely to be stereotypically attractive so they were unjustifiably placed at a disadvantage (i.e. indirect discrimination). It might also be argued that the claimant had made an allegation of discrimination before the decision was made about which members of staff should be front-of-house, and it is therefore also possible that the employer decided not to give this particular employee a place at front-of-house in retaliation for the discrimination complaint (i.e. victimisation). Unless it is not clear to the employee which of the four claims (direct age discrimination/age-related harassment/indirect discrimination/victimisation) are most likely to succeed, pleading all four might undermine the strongest claim. If the claimant is trying to persuade a tribunal that the treatment was because of age, it might be undermining for the tribunal to consider whether there was another cause, like the discrimination complaint in a victimisation claim. Tribunals sometimes express frustration at having to determine four legal claims when it is obvious that one, over the others, is the most likely to be upheld, and it would have been simpler to have only pursued that claim. A claimant would be well-advised to consider at an early stage what the evidence is likely to be. If there is already evidence that age was a relevant causative factor for the treatment, there is little point constructing an indirect discrimination claim or victimisation in the alternative.

Defending an ET claim

The claim form will be sent to the respondent(s) by the ET. Once it is received the respondent usually has 28 days to respond. The response must be given in an ET3 form. This form is available here:

https://assets.publishing.service.gov.uk/media/65bcbec74a666f0010174 7b6/ET3_0224.pdf

If it is going to be impossible for the respondent to respond within 28 days, the respondent or their representative should apply, preferably within the time limit, to the ET for an extension of time to file a response by explaining why it is impossible to comply with the usual deadline.

The ET3 form itself is straightforward to complete. It is important for the employer/respondent to set out where it agrees and disagrees with the claimant, whether it concedes the claims and, if not, why not. Along with the basic information, Section 6 of the ET3 should be completed to detail the grounds on which the claim is contested. It is often the case that more space is required to do this and a separate document called "Grounds of Resistance" is attached to the ET3 form.

An example of a simple Grounds of Resistance in response to a fictional age discrimination case (set out in the example Particulars of Claim at Appendix 1) is set out at Appendix 2.

If a claim is not responded to within the time allowed, a judgment in default is usually entered pursuant to Rule 22 ET Rules. If a determination can be made on the papers without a hearing, the ET will make it, otherwise there will be a hearing. The respondent is only allowed to participate in future proceedings to the extent allowed by the ET in the interests of justice.

Preliminary hearings

Most discrimination cases, except the most simple, need to be case managed by a judge at a hearing. A case management hearing is a private hearing (i.e. one where the public are not permitted to observe), usually undertaken remotely (by telephone or by video) and consists of the judge and parties working together to identify the steps which need to be taken for the matter to be heard at a trial. Each party must come prepared to discuss how the matter will be heard. The ET has a proforma document always sent to the parties before a preliminary hearing for case management called the Case Management Agenda. It is important to complete this as far as possible as it sets out all matters likely to be discussed at the preliminary hearing. The form can be seen here:

https://www.judiciary.uk/wp-content/uploads/2024/11/Agenda-for-Case-Management-England-Wales-English-PDF-version-1.pdf?mc_cid=edd4844cfa&mc_eid=ab60e5a8a1

One of the most important parts of a case management hearing, is to identify a list of issues for the full hearing. This is a list of questions which will need to be answered by the tribunal to determine all the claims pursued. This list usually limits the points to be considered at the full hearing, so it is important to include all the issues at this stage. The version of the Agenda which was updated on 1st November 2024 (as in the link above) includes a note that states only legally represented parties should complete the list of issues box. The Agenda might also be a good opportunity to include extra information on the claim which is not contained in the claim form, or to request extra information from the other party. The Court of Appeal explored the status of a list of issues in ***Parekh v London Borough of Brent*** [2012] EWCA Civ 1630, CA, see also ***Bogdan v Cabinet Office – Government Digital Services*** [2024] EAT 177.

An example of a list of issues (for the fictional case set out in Appendices 1 and 2) is at Appendix 3.

A closed/private preliminary hearing can deal with applications to amend the claim form or response, a request for further information from the other party, requests for another preliminary hearing, and directions for trial. Trial directions typically include dates for disclosure (where each party exchanges relevant documents with the other); for the production of a "bundle" (the paginated and indexed file of all documents to which the ET will be referred at trial); for the exchange of witness statements (the statements of all the evidence of all witnesses to be called by either party); and the listing of the full hearing (how many days will be required to hear all the evidence, submissions from both sides, for the ET to deliberate and give a judgment? When can the ET schedule that time?).

Applications to amend should be made in writing where reasonably possible, with the proposed amendment itself also being set out in writing. The parties should bear in mind that if reference to a general claim of "*age discrimination*" is included in an ET1, that does not incorporate any claim for direct/indirect discrimination/harassment or victimisation (see ***Quarcoopome v Sock Shop Holdings Ltd*** [1995] IRLR

353, EAT) so will probably need to be particularised, with permission from the tribunal.

The Presidential Guidance on General Case Management for England and Wales (published on 13 March 2014, and amended and reissued on 22 January 2018) gives guidance on how an application to amend should be considered. The core test has been described by HHJ Tayler in ***Vaughan v Modality Partnership*** [2021] ICR 535, EAT as the balance of injustice and hardship in allowing or refusing the application.

Sometimes an open (public) preliminary hearing will be scheduled. This is normally to determine a point which could mean a claim or claims come to an end, like a strike-out application.

Under Rule 38 ET Rules, an ET may strike out a claim or response but in reality, it is rare for discrimination claims to be struck out at a preliminary stage on the grounds that it has no reasonable prospects of success (under Rule 38(1)(a) ET Rules), because the claims tend to be very dependent upon the factual findings of the tribunal having heard all the evidence. In an example of such a rare case in the age discrimination context, the EAT have endorsed strike out, where the difference in age between the claimant and the comparator was only nine months, on the basis that prospects of success of demonstrating facts from which discrimination could be inferred were "*fanciful*" – ***ABN AMRO Management Services Ltd and anor v Hogben*** EAT 0266/09.

In relation to limitation on age discrimination claims (to be determined pursuant to s.123 EqA), tribunals usually prefer to determine at a full (final) hearing, rather than at a preliminary stage, questions of:

(a) whether there was a course of discriminatory conduct over time, especially where the claimant alleges that the course of conduct ended within three months of the claim form being presented;

(b) whether it is just and equitable to extend time for earlier alleged acts of discrimination, where there are some claims based on later alleged acts of discrimination which are in time.

Privacy and restrictions on disclosure in proceedings

Given that any open preliminary hearings and full hearings are heard in public, sometimes a party wishes to make an application to restrict the reporting of certain aspects of the case. Rule 49 of the ET Rules states:

> *(1) The Tribunal may, on its own initiative or on the application of a party, make an order with a view to preventing or restricting the public disclosure of any aspect of proceedings so far as it considers necessary in the interests of justice or in order to protect the Convention rights of any person.*
>
> *(2) In considering whether to make an order under this rule, the Tribunal must give full weight to the principle of open justice and to the Convention right to freedom of expression.*
>
> *(3) Any order made under this rule may require—*
>
> > *(a) that a hearing that would otherwise be held in public be conducted, in whole or in part, in private;*
> >
> > *(b) that the identities of specified parties, witnesses or other persons referred to in the proceedings should not be disclosed to the public, by the use of anonymisation or otherwise, whether in the course of any hearing or in its listing or in any documents entered on the Register or otherwise forming part of the public record;*
> >
> > *(c) that measures are to be taken to prevent witnesses at a public hearing being identifiable by members of the public;*
> >
> > *(d) that a restricted reporting order is in place within the terms of section 11 (restriction of publicity in cases involving sexual*

misconduct) or 12 (restriction of publicity in disability cases) of the Employment Tribunals Act;

(e) that the name, address or other information of, or relating to, any person be redacted from a claim form, response form, witness statement or any other document in the proceedings.

(4) Any party, or other person with a legitimate interest, who has not had a reasonable opportunity to make representations before an order under this rule is made may apply to the *Tribunal in writing for the order to be revoked or discharged, either on the basis of written representations or, if requested, at a hearing.*

(5) Where an order is of the kind mentioned in paragraph (3)(d), the order—

(a) must specify the person whose identity is protected,

(b) must specify the duration of the order,

(c) may specify particular matters of which publication is prohibited as likely to lead to that person's identification, and

(d) may specify that it also applies to any other proceedings.

(6) The Tribunal must ensure that a notice that an order has been made under this rule in respect of particular proceedings is displayed on the notice board of the Tribunal with any list of the proceedings taking place before the Tribunal, and on the door of the room in which the proceedings affected by the order are taking place.

(7) "Convention rights" has the meaning given to it in section 1 of the Human Rights Act 1998(1).

The presumption is always that there should be open justice and so an applicant for an order under Rule 49 will have to convince a tribunal that there are very good reasons to depart from that principle – ***Ameyaw v***

PricewaterhouseCoopers Services Ltd [2019] ICR 976, EAT. The EAT recently considered the authorities in relation to privacy in ET proceedings and anonymity orders in ***XY v AB*** 2025 EAT 66. Litigants and practitioners are encouraged to refer to these authorities as the detail relating to Rule 49 is outside the scope of this book.

The Full Hearing in the ET

Usually a full ET panel of three members including a judge, would hear claims of age discrimination, but from 29th October 2024, a judge can decide, having regard to the interests of justice and the overriding objective, whether an ET is to consist of a judge sitting alone or a full panel including lay members (see Practice Direction on panel composition in the Employment Tribunals and Employment Appeal Tribunal – October 2024 and Joint Presidential Guidance on panel composition in the Employment Tribunals – October 2024).

Full Hearings are generally held in public. The procedure is usually that the tribunal will discuss the issues and timetable initially with the parties. The parties should know whether the tribunal intend to deal with liability only (the question of whether or not the claims will succeed) or liability and remedy (what compensation or other remedy should be awarded). The tribunal tend then to take some time to read a selection of the most relevant documents (including the pleadings and the witness statements at least). Once the hearing resumes, usually the claimant's evidence in a discrimination claim will go first, because the claimant has the primary burden of proof. Each of the witnesses will be called, asked to confirm that their witness statement is true, after promising to tell the truth, and then the witness will be cross-examined by the other parties (or their representatives) and the tribunal will also ask any questions they may have. There is then an opportunity for the witness's party's representative to ask questions in re-examination. This is only permitted to include questions arising from the witness's answers in cross-examination and the questions must not be leading (suggesting the answer). After all of the parties' witnesses have given evidence, the parties (or their representatives) will be asked to give closing submissions, which is a speech summarising the claims, the evidence and the law from that party's perspective, with the aim of persuading the tribunal to uphold or dismiss the claims. Usually there will be a period of time when the tribunal will deliberate and consider its judgment before judgment is given, sometimes orally in the tribunal room. Sometimes judgment is reserved, which means it will be given in writing and sent to the parties.

ET judgments are published online. Where written reasons are given by the ET, that is, the detailed explanation of all the findings of the tribunal, those written reasons are also published online. Both parties should bear in mind that the ET's findings about the case will be searchable by any member of the public once the written reasons are given. This might include embarrassing details which the parties would prefer to keep private, and might not have been heard by anyone not involved in the case when the matter was heard in the ET. Avoiding a public judgment (and/or written reasons) is often a key motivation to settle before the ET makes any final determinations.

Unlike the position in the civil courts, where usually the unsuccessful party pays the costs of the successful party, costs orders are rare in the ET system. The only circumstances in which costs orders can be made are set out in rr.72-82 ET Rules. It is possible for a party who has not been represented to claim a "preparation time order" on the same principles.

Enforcement of awards

Once the ET has given a judgment, including on remedy, that is, the award that is payable if the claimant succeeds (see Chapter 9 Remedy), the award is usually payable by the respondent within 14 days (Employment Tribunal Procedure Rules 2024, Rule 64). For claims presented on or after 29 July 2013, interest begins to accrue from the day immediately following the date on which the original ET judgment was sent to the parties. However, no interest is payable if the full amount of the award is paid within 14 days of the judgment being sent. The rate of interest applied is set by the Judgments Act 1838 and is currently 8%.

If the award is not paid by the respondent, a claimant can:

- Enforce the judgment through ACAS and ET fast track enforcement procedure, which is a streamlined process for enforcing tribunal awards.

- File a copy of the ET judgment with the county court so it can be entered on the Register of Judgments, Orders and Fines, making it enforceable as a County Court Order. The county court can then use various enforcement methods such as a warrant of control, an attachment of earnings order, a third-party debt order, a charging order, or bankruptcy proceedings to recover the debt.

- Submit a Penalty Enforcement Form to the Department for Business and Trade, which will then issue a warning notice to the employer, giving them 28 days to pay the outstanding amount. If the employer fails to pay within this period, a penalty notice can be issued, imposing a financial penalty of 50% of the outstanding amount, subject to a minimum of £100 and a maximum of £5,000. This can include a public "naming and shaming" in a quarterly press release on gov.uk. Any penalty is payable to the government, not the claimant.

- Initiate insolvency proceedings, though this only covers awards of £5,000 or more and preferential and secured creditors will take priority so the prospects of recovery are relatively low. An application to the National Insurance Fund can be made when the respondent is insolvent but only covers redundancy payments or basic award, arrears of pay between 1 and 8 weeks, pay for a statutory minimum period of notice, and some holiday pay claims. The Fund does not pay claims for injury to feelings awards.

Appeals from the ET

The procedure of the Employment Appeal Tribunal ("EAT") is governed by the Employment Appeal Tribunal Rules 1993 SI 1993/2854 ('the EAT Rules') and the various EAT Practice Directions. Litigants dealing with appeals should consult these as a detailed description of the procedure is outside the scope of this book.

Any appeal must be lodged using Form 1, 1A or 2 (or substantially in accordance with those forms) – rule 3(1)(a) of the EAT Rules. Certain documents must be lodged at the same time to institute the appeal. From 1st February 2025, it is now permissible for legally represented parties to e-file an appeal – (see rule 35 of the EAT Rules and the Employment Appeal Tribunal (Amendment) Rules 2024 SI 2024/1044).

The appeal must be instituted within 42 days from the date on which the written record of the judgment was sent to the parties (r. 3(3)(a)(i) EAT Rules), or within 42 days of the written reasons for the judgment ("WR") being sent to the parties if (a) the WR were requested orally at the hearing, (b) WR were requested in writing within 14 days of the written record of the judgment, (c) WR were requested out of time but granted, or (d) where the ET itself reserved its reasons and gave them subsequently. The date on which the record or WR is sent is not counted in the calculation of 42 days, so, if the record of judgment is sent on a Tuesday, the appeal must be instituted by 4pm on the Tuesday, six weeks later. Where the deadline falls on a bank holiday, time is extended to the next day the EAT office is open. When appealing an order or other type of decision (e.g. from a preliminary hearing) time starts to run from the date of the order, irrespective of whether WR are provided.

Under r.37(1) EAT Rules the time prescribed for doing any act may be extended. Although minor errors may be overlooked and time extended to enable correction, it is generally quite difficult to obtain an extension of time to institute an appeal. Any litigant looking to persuade the EAT to extend time should consult the Court of Appeal judgment in ***Ridley v HB Kirtley t/a Queen's Court Business Centre*** [2024] IRLR 845 and the judgment of Eady P in ***AB v The University of East London*** [2024] EAT 157 (27 September 2024, unreported).

Appeals to the EAT only lie in errors of law, which means that the EAT will not normally re-examine issues of fact. The grounds of the appeal should be set out concisely, numbered and must identify the error of law relied upon. The 2023 Practice Direction (which came into force on 30 September 2023) should be consulted as to what constitutes *grounds of appeal* (particularly paragraph 3.8).

Any party seeking to appeal a judgment should generally try to identify and articulate in their Notice of Appeal at least one of the following:

- How the ET applied the wrong legal test or incorrectly applied the correct legal test;

- That the ET reached a decision of fact for which there was no evidence, or reached a decision no reasonable tribunal could have reached, i.e. the decision was perverse. It is not enough to assert that a factual finding was contrary to some, or even most, of the evidence. The threshold to establish perversity is set extremely high (see ***Yeboah v Crofton*** [2002] IRLR 634).

- That the ET failed to take into account a relevant matter or took into account an irrelevant matter. The appellant must identify the relevant matter that was overlooked or the irrelevant matter that was considered.

- That the ET decided a point that was not argued, or gave reasons that do not enable a party to understand why they lost.

- That the ET did not follow the correct procedure in a way that affected the outcome, or conducted the hearing in an unfair way. This generally requires evidence to be given by the appellant or a person present at the hearing. If a party is alleging bias or procedural impropriety, the procedures set out at section 3.10 EAT Practice Direction 2023 must be complied with.

If the appellant does not properly particularise the appeal, it is likely to be rejected by the EAT (see ***Tran v Greenwich Vietnam Community Project*** EAT 185/00).

Appeals are processed through a sift. What this means is that if it is not clear that there was arguably an error of law made by the tribunal which is of practical significance, and therefore it appears that there are no reasonable grounds for bringing the appeal, it will be rejected on paper pursuant to rule 3(7) EAT Rules. The appellant will then usually have the opportunity (within 28 days from the date the Registrar sent the notification of rejection) to request an oral hearing (which usually does not involve the respondent to the appeal) to seek to persuade a judge that there is an arguable ground of appeal (pursuant to rule 3(10) EAT Rules, paras.4.4.2 and 4.4.3 of the 2023 Practice Direction). Sometimes, if the Registrar or judge considers that the notice of appeal is totally without merit the appellant will not be entitled to an oral hearing, in which case the only recourse would be to appeal to the Court of Appeal (rule 3(7ZA) EAT Rules).

Once an appeal has proceeded through the sift (either after a decision on paper that the appeal can proceed or after a Rule 3(10) hearing) the respondent is required to submit a response, known as 'an Answer' to the appeal. Usually this must be done within 28 days from the seal date of the EAT Order to lodge an Answer. The Answer should be in accordance with Form 3 (which will be sent out with the EAT Order). The Answer should set out whether the appeal is resisted, and if so, on what grounds. It is possible for a respondent to lodge a cross-appeal, at the time of lodging the Answer. The same sift process applies to cross-appeals (under rules 6(12)-(16) EAT Rules).

The EAT can order preliminary hearings to take place, usually with both parties. It can also exercise various case management powers, similar to the ET, including giving witness orders, ordering joinder of parties, amending notices of appeal/cross-appeals or a respondent's answer, waiving rules, extending time, postponing hearings, expediting appeals, appointing a litigation friend, making anonymity and restricted reporting orders, and obtaining enhanced written reasons from the ET (known as the *Burns/Barke* procedure – see Rule 60(5) ET Rules and s.8.11 2023 Practice Direction).

Where a party to the appeal considers that a point of law cannot be argued without reference to evidence given (or not given) at the ET, an application should be made to the EAT (see s.8.10 of 2023 Practice Direction). Often parties will be ordered to cooperate to agree a note of the evidence given to the ET. There are very limited circumstances in which a party can rely in the EAT on evidence *not* before the ET (see s.8.12 of 2023 Practice Direction). Generally an argument not advanced before the ET cannot be advanced on appeal (see s.8.13 of 2023 Practice Direction).

Preparation for appeal hearings is usually directed by the EAT through orders given once the respondent's Answer has been submitted. Usually the parties will be directed to agree what documents are necessary to be referred to, and a core bundle (and perhaps also a supplementary bundle) of documents should be produced for use at the hearing (it is essential that parties consult the 2023 Practice Direction at sections 11.3 – 11.4 in relation to documents). The production of skeleton arguments for each side of the appeal is also almost always necessary (s.11.6 of the 2023 Practice Direction should be consulted). Usually skeleton arguments are required to be submitted and exchanged with the other side 14 days before the hearing, and authorities cited should be collated into a bundle and sent to the EAT 7 days before the hearing (see s.11.7 of the 2023 Practice Direction). Generally, the number of authorities cited should be restricted to 10, unless it is an exceptionally complex appeal.

<u>Appeal beyond the Employment Appeal Tribunal</u>

To appeal from a decision of the EAT in England and Wales, the usual route is to the Court of Appeal. This appeal can only be made on a point of law and requires permission either from the EAT or the Court of Appeal. The application for permission to appeal should be made to the EAT at the hearing if an oral judgment is given, or in writing within seven days thereafter. If a written judgment is handed down, the application should be made to the EAT when it is handed down or in writing within seven days thereafter. If applying directly to the Court of Appeal, the application must be made within 21 days of the date the order was sealed.

APPENDIX A

All names are fictional and the factual information is imagined. Any resemblance to any real people or events is entirely coincidental.

IN THE [CENTRAL LONDON] EMPLOYMENT TRIBUNAL **Case no.: 1231234/2025**

B E T W E E N :

Ms JACQUELINE SMITH

Claimant

-and-

MGKMRT LTD

First Respondent

Ms NINA BLACK

Second Respondent

PARTICULARS OF CLAIM

The parties

1. The First Respondent is a ladies' fashion retail brand based in central London, with four retail outlets in the Greater London area. The First Respondent's flagship store is located at 1 Regent Street, London, W1B ("the Flagship Store").

2. The Claimant began her fashion retail career in 2002. She worked in a number of well-renowned fashion retail stores and became a retail manager in or around 2015. The Claimant has managed a number of flagship fashion stores in Central London since then. The Claimant's employment with the First Respondent began on 1st June 2023 as a store manager of the Clapham High Street store ("the Clapham Store").

3. The Second Respondent was employed by the First Respondent from September 2024 as the new Area Manager and became the Claimant's line manager from September 2024 onwards. The Claimant's employment was terminated with effect from 28th March 2025 by reason of her discriminatory constructive dismissal.

4. The Claimant was 45 years old at the time of her constructive dismissal. The Second Respondent was 26 years old.

The claims and the Respondents' liability

5. The Claimant brings the following claims:

   5.1 Direct age discrimination, contrary to s.13 Equality Act 2010 ("EqA");

   5.2 Harassment related to age, contrary to s.26 EqA;

   5.3 Indirect age discrimination, contrary to s.19 EqA;

   5.4 Victimisation, contrary to s.27 EqA.

6. From September 2024 onwards, the First Respondent, as the Claimant's employer, discriminated against, harassed and victimised the Claimant, subjecting her to various detriments and constructively dismissing her, contrary to ss.39-40 EqA. The Second Respondent, in the course of her employment by the First Respondent, discriminated against, harassed and victimised the Claimant and caused the Claimant's constructive dismissal, contrary to s.110(1) EqA. The First Respondent is vicariously liable for the discriminatory actions of the Second Respondent, according to s.109(1) EqA.

7. The Respondents' discriminatory course of conduct began in September 2024 and continued until the effective date of termination of the Claimant's employment on 28th March 2025. The Claimant began ACAS Early Conciliation on 2nd June 2025 and the certificate was issued on 10th June 2025. The Claimant presented her claims on 27th June 2025. The claims were therefore presented within three months of the discriminatory acts (or of the end of the period over which the discriminatory conduct extended), as specified by s.123 EqA.

<u>Background to the claims</u>

8. The Claimant passed her probationary period in September 2023 and was given an excellent appraisal rating in December 2023. The Claimant had a good professional relationship with her line manager, the Area Manager, Mr Milo Jackson, and the shop assistants at the Clapham Store.

9. In or around July 2024, Mr Jackson told the Claimant he was leaving the First Respondent's employment, and he knew that the manager of the Flagship Store, Ms Claire Haines, was also leaving in the next six months, so there would be a management vacancy at the Flagship Store. Mr Jackson told the Claimant that the management role at the Flagship Store attracted a greater salary than the management role of the Clapham Store, due to

the public prominence of the position within the First Respondent and greater media exposure. He also advised the Claimant that she should apply for the management role at the Flagship Store because she was the most qualified and well-suited internal candidate.

10. From September 2024, the First Respondent recruited a new Area Manager, Nina Black (the Second Respondent). The Second Respondent became the Claimant's new line manager. The Second Respondent was considerably younger and less experienced than the Claimant in the retail sector. The Second Respondent had enjoyed some success as a fashion social media "*influencer*" and was brought in by the First Respondent to inject some youth into the retail operation.

The Second Respondent's discriminatory conduct

11. From the moment the Second Respondent arrived, she made clear to the Claimant that the Respondents considered her too old for a prominent position within the First Respondent's business.

12. On 25th September 2024 the Claimant met the Second Respondent for the first time at a meeting at the Clapham Store. The Second Respondent did a presentation and said that her introduction to the business meant "*It's out with the old, and in with the new!*". She said the First Respondent brand was old and tired and needed to be reinvigorated with "*new Gen Z energy*". Although the Claimant tried to sound enthusiastic, she was concerned that the new image of the First Respondent did not include her. The comments made by the Second Respondent on 25th September 2024 were unwanted, clearly related to age and they had the purpose or effect of violating the Claimant's dignity, and/or creating an intimidating, hostile, degrading, humiliating or offensive environment for the Claimant.

13. The next time the Claimant saw the Second Respondent, the Second Respondent visited the Clapham Store on 15th October 2024. The Claimant's shift started at 10.30am and the Second Respondent was already at the store when she arrived. When the Claimant walked through the door, the Second Respondent shrieked "*Oh my God, Jackie, you look like such a Granny in that outfit!*". The Claimant was very embarrassed and was humiliated in front of the other members of staff, one of whom giggled under her breath.

14. On the 20th November 2024 the Claimant had to attend an Area Sales meeting at the Flagship Store. The Second Respondent gave a speech which included encouraging the stores managers, including the Claimant, to dissuade older customers from browsing the stores. The Second Respondent said "*We don't want a load of geriatrics damaging the brand*".

15. On 15th December 2024, the Claimant had her annual appraisal with the Second Respondent. The Clapham Store had been the best performing store the First Respondent had in 2024. The staff turnover was very low because the Claimant's relationships with everyone were so good. The Claimant deserved to have a repeated excellent performance rating, like the previous year.

16. Unfortunately, the Second Respondent took the opportunity unjustifiably to criticise the Claimant's performance and conduct at work. The Second Respondent said she was too slow to accept change, was obstructive and difficult to work with. She said the Claimant was "*stuck in your ways*" and she had to keep up with her young staff. To her shock, the Claimant was given a rating of "Below expectations". As a consequence of that rating the Claimant did not receive a Christmas bonus of £500. Later that month, the Claimant spoke to her colleague, Elise Cole, who manages one of the First Respondent's stores located in Notting Hill, and has worked for the First Respondent for less than a year, about her bonus. Ms Cole received an Excellent rating, despite

the fact her store did not perform as well as the Clapham Store. Ms Cole described the Second Respondent's appraisal of her as "*gushing*". Ms Cole was aged 32 years at the time.

<u>The Instagram Bonus Scheme</u>

17. On 1st February 2025, the First Respondent announced a new bonus scheme for employees. Every month from 1st March 2025, the top 5 employees with the most "likes" on Instagram for a post showing the First Respondent's clothes or name, would receive a bonus of £100 ("the Instagram Bonus Scheme"). The Claimant, as an older employee, did not have an Instagram account, and did not know how to set one up. Her colleagues, who were mostly under the age of 35 years, all already had established Instagram accounts with a lot of followers. The Claimant could not compete. Inevitably, on 1st March 2025, the Claimant was not eligible for a bonus and was unlikely to be eligible in the future. Five of her colleagues received a bonus. All of these colleagues were in their 20s or 30s. Again, the Claimant felt isolated and alienated because of her age.

<u>The application for the Flagship Store</u>

18. In early January 2025, the Claimant saw an advertisement on the First Respondent's website for the role of manager at the Flagship Store. The advertised salary was £50,000 pa, which was £10,000 higher than the Claimant's salary. The Claimant applied, knowing that she was the most experienced manager of any of the First Respondent's stores. Unfortunately, on 20th February 2025 she was interviewed by the Second Respondent. Despite the Second Respondent's obvious hostility towards her, the Claimant interviewed well and was optimistic about her prospects of success.

19. On 18th March 2025, the Claimant was informed by letter that she had been unsuccessful in her application. The letter, written

by the Second Respondent, stated that she lacked "*dynamism*" the First Respondent was looking for, to respond to "*rapidly changing times*". On 20th March 2025, the Claimant learned that the new manager of the flagship store was the 27 year-old Marcia Hillier, who was an external candidate. Ms Hillier had very little retail experience, and no management experience. The Claimant was objectively a better candidate for the job than her but had been passed over for the promotion because of her greater age.

The second Respondent's retaliation

20. On 20th March 2025, the Claimant sent a grievance to the First Respondent, setting out the age discrimination and harassment she had suffered in her role since the Second Respondent had started her employment. The grievance was a protected act under s.27(2)(d) EqA. The First Respondent ignored the grievance completely and took no action in response to it.

21. On 25th March 2025, the Second Respondent visited the Clapham Store, on the Claimant's day off. The Second Respondent ripped down the window merchandising which the Claimant had taken many hours to present the previous week, and was heard by one of the Claimant's colleagues to have muttered, "*That'll teach her not to make nasty complaints about me!*"

The Claimant's constructive dismissal

22. On 28th March 2025, when the Claimant next attended work, she was devastated to see that her work on merchandising had been destroyed by the Second Respondent. It was the last straw.

23. The Claimant could no longer work for the First Respondent, with the Second Respondent. She had no trust or confidence that the First Respondent would do anything to prevent the discrimination, harassment and victimisation from continuing.

The Claimant decided to accept the First Respondent's breach of her contract of employment and considered herself constructively dismissed. She emailed her resignation with immediate effect to the First Respondent that afternoon.

24. The effective date of termination of her contract of employment was the 28th March 2025.

The claims

Harassment – s.26 EqA

25. The Second Respondent's comments:

25.1 on 25th September 2024: "*It's out with the old, and in with the new!*"; criticising the First Respondent brand for being old and tired; referring to needing reinvigoration with "*new Gen Z energy*";

25.2 on 15th October 2024, "*Oh my God, Jackie, you look like such a Granny in that outfit!*";

25.3 on the 20th November 2024 instructions to dissuade older customers from browsing the stores and saying "*We don't want a load of geriatrics damaging the brand*";

25.4 on 15th December 2024 saying the Claimant was too slow to accept change, was obstructive and difficult to work with; "*stuck in your ways*" and she had to keep up with her young staff;

25.5 the 18th March 2025 letter stating the Claimant lacked the "*dynamism*" the First Respondent was looking for to respond to "*rapidly changing times*";

were unwanted, clearly related to age and they had the purpose or effect of violating the Claimant's dignity, and/or creating an intimidating, hostile, degrading, humiliating or offensive environment for the Claimant. The Second Respondent's comments therefore constituted harassment related to age, contrary to s.26 EqA.

Direct age discrimination – s.13 EqA

26. The Claimant was treated in the following ways:

    26.1 given an appraisal rating of "Below expectations" on 15th December 2024, rather than the "Excellent" rating which she deserved, contrary to the treatment of a hypothetical comparator under the age of 35 years, or of Elise Cole;

    26.2 not being paid the £500 Christmas bonus, contrary to the treatment of a hypothetical comparator under the age of 35 years, or of Elise Cole;

    26.3 not being appointed the manager of the Flagship Store, contrary to the treatment of a hypothetical comparator under the age of 35 years, or of Marcia Hillier;

    26.4 being constructively dismissed on 28th March 2025.

27. The Claimant's treatment was because she was over the age of 40 years, and constituted less favourable treatment than a hypothetical person under the age of 35 years, or the actual comparators named above. This was therefore direct age discrimination contrary to s.13 EqA.

Indirect age discrimination – s.19 EqA

28. The First Respondent's Instagram Bonus Scheme was a provision, criterion or practice which was applied to all employees of all ages, but it placed, or would place, older employees of over the age of 40 years at a particular disadvantage because the older employees were less likely than the employees

under 35 years, to have an Instagram account, established or at all. The introduction of the Instagram Bonus Scheme put the Claimant at a disadvantage in comparison to her younger colleagues (under the age of 35 years). The First Respondent cannot show that it was a proportionate means of achieving a legitimate aim.

Victimisation – s.27 EqA

29. The Claimant did a protected act, as defined by s.27(2)(d) EqA by raising a grievance on 20th March 2025. The Second Respondent destroyed the Claimant's window merchandising on 25th March 2025 because of the Claimant's protected act, or because she believed the Claimant had done or may do a protected act. The Claimant was therefore victimised, contrary to s.27 EqA.

Remedy

30. As a result of the discrimination, harassment and victimisation the Claimant suffered between September 2024 and 28th March 2025 and her discriminatory constructive dismissal, the Claimant suffered considerable loss and damage, including:

30.1 Loss of bonus of £500 in Christmas 2024;

30.2 Loss of bonus from the Instagram Bonus Scheme from 1st March 2025;

30.3 Loss of payrise (to £50,000 pa) associated with the promotion which the Claimant should have been offered in or around March 2025;

30.4 Loss of earnings flowing from her constructive dismissal, which is continuing because the Claimant has been unable to find another job yet;

30.5 Injury to feelings;

30.6 Interest.

31. The First Respondent unreasonably failed to follow the ACAS Code of Practice on Disciplinary and Grievance Procedures by ignoring the Claimant's grievance dated the 20th March 2025. The Claimant is entitled to an uplift in any compensation found to be payable to her of up to 25%, pursuant to s.207A Trade Union and Labour Relations (Consolidation) Act 1992

32. A Schedule of Loss will be served at the appropriate time.

AND the Claimant claims:

(a) a Declaration that she has been discriminated against within the meaning of s.124(2)(a) EqA, and/or

(b) a Recommendation pursuant to s.124(2)(c) EqA, and/or

(c) an award for injury to feelings pursuant to s.119(4) EqA, and/or

(d) compensation for loss of earnings (including future loss of earnings) pursuant to s.124(2)(b) EqA, and/or

(e) an ACAS uplift pursuant to section 207A of the Trade Union and Labour Relations (Consolidation) Act 1992, and/or

(f) interest pursuant to The Employment Tribunals (Interests on Awards in Discrimination Cases) Regulations 1996 SI 1996/2803, and/or

(g) any other loss that flows from the Respondents' treatment of her pursuant to s.124(2)(b) EqA.

[NAME OF CLAIMANT or REPRESENTATIVE]

[DATE]

APPENDIX B

All names are fictional and the factual information is imagined. Any resemblance to any real people or events is entirely coincidental.

IN THE [CENTRAL LONDON] EMPLOYMENT TRIBUNAL

Case no.: 1231234/2025

B E T W E E N :

Ms JACQUELINE SMITH

Claimant

-and-

MGKMRT LTD

First Respondent

Ms NINA BLACK

Second Respondent

GROUNDS OF RESISTANCE

---

1. These Grounds of Resistance are submitted on behalf of both Respondents in response to the claims presented by the Claimant on 27th June 2025 in case number 1231234/2025. All claims are vehemently denied by both Respondents. The claims brought by the Claimant are understood to be of:

    1.1 Direct age discrimination, contrary to s.13 Equality Act 2010 ("EqA");

    1.2 Harassment related to age, contrary to s.26 EqA;

    1.3 Indirect age discrimination, contrary to s.19 EqA;

    1.4 Victimisation, contrary to s.27 EqA.

2. The First Respondent is a feminine fashion retailer with a nationally-recognised brand and excellent reputation in cutting-edge curation. The First Respondent employed the Claimant from 1st June 2023 until her resignation with immediate effect on 28th March 2025. The First Respondent also employed the Second Respondent from 1st September 2024 and continuing. The Claimant was employed as manager of the First Respondent's retail store in Clapham High Street ("the Clapham Store"). The Second Respondent is employed as the Area Manager and was the Claimant line manager.

3. The Claimant was not a victim of age discrimination, of any kind, including harassment and victimisation, at any point during her employment with the First Respondent. It became clear, during her relatively short employment that she was ill-suited to the fast-moving fashion retail industry.

<u>Preliminary issues</u>

4. The First Respondent accepts that it would be liable under ss.39-40 EqA as the Claimant's employer, for any alleged

discriminatory acts (including harassment and victimisation) during the course of the Claimant's employment, which are denied, that are upheld by the tribunal. The First Respondent also concedes that it is vicariously liable, pursuant to s.109(1) EqA, for the conduct of the Second Respondent, in the course of her employment, to the extent that any unlawful conduct, which is denied, is upheld by the tribunal. The First Respondent confirms that it is not seeking to rely upon the statutory defence in s.109(4) EqA in respect of the Second Respondent's actions or omissions.

5. Many of the Claimant's claims were presented outside of the primary time limit set out at s.123 EqA and are outside the jurisdiction of the employment tribunal. The Claimant began ACAS Early Conciliation on 2nd June 2025 and the certificate was issued on 10th June 2025. The Claimant presented her claims on 27th June 2025. Any claim complaining of events which took place on or before the 2nd March 2025 is *prima facie* out of time, and it is not just and equitable to extend time. The Respondents deny that there was any course of discriminatory conduct which extended over time (or at all) and the tribunal is invited to find that limitation had expired in relation to many of the claims before they were presented.

Response to the Particulars of Claim

6. Except where the contrary is indicated, the below reference to paragraph numbers is a reference to the numbered paragraphs of the Particulars of Claim attached to the claim form submitted by the Claimant.

7. Paragraph 1 is admitted.

8. Paragraph 2 is admitted to the extent it is within the knowledge of the Respondents. According to the Claimant's application to the First Respondent, the Claimant had experience in the retail

industry dating back to 2002, including managing two flagship fashion stores in London. The Claimant did not, prior to her employment with the First Respondent, have any experience of managing premium, carefully-curated fashion stores.

9. Paragraphs 3 and 4 are admitted, except that it is denied that the Claimant was constructively dismissed and/or discriminated against. The Claimant's employment was terminated by resignation.

10. Subject to the points made above in relation to limitation and jurisdiction, paragraph 5 is admitted.

11. Except as set out in paragraph 4 of Grounds of Resistance above, paragraph 6 is denied.

12. In relation to paragraph 7, it is denied that there were any discriminatory acts and/or a discriminatory course of conduct, though it is admitted that the Claimant alleges discrimination occurred from September 2024 until her employment with the First Respondent ended. It is denied that the claims were presented in time, except to the extent a complaint relates to the period from 3rd March 2025 onwards. All claims about treatment or conduct allegedly occurring on or before 2nd March 2025 are outside of the primary time limit and it is not just and equitable to extend time under s.123 EqA.

Background to the claims

13. Paragraph 8 is admitted insofar as the Claimant did pass her probationary period in September 2023 with an excellent appraisal rating. It is denied that the Claimant had a professional relationship with Mr Jackson, the then Area Manager for the First Respondent – Mr Jackson and the Claimant had a close personal friendship, which explains the excellent rating despite the fact that the Clapham Store was underperforming. It is denied that

the Claimant had a good relationship, professional or at all with the shop assistants at the Clapham Store.

14. Neither Respondent was party to the conversation referred to in paragraph 9 and so the alleged content of the conversation is neither admitted nor denied. To the extent it is relevant, the Claimant is required to prove such assertions. For the avoidance of doubt it is admitted that the manager position of the Flagship Store normally attracts a higher salary than management positions in the other First Respondent stores. Ms Haines did not submit her resignation from the management position at the Flagship Store until early October 2024. Whatever Mr Jackson told the Claimant, it is not true that the Claimant was the most qualified and well-suited internal candidate for the Flagship Store manager role.

15. In relation to paragraph 10, the first two sentences are admitted and it is admitted that the Second Respondent was 26 years old at the time of the First Respondent's recruitment of her, and therefore considerably younger than the Claimant who was 45 years old at the time. The rest of the paragraph is denied. The Second Respondent had more relevant experience than the Claimant in the premium fashion retail sector, in that the Second Respondent was previously an "Instagram ambassador", for another premium fashion brand, and had also run a carefully curated fashion boutique and fashion brand of her own. It is specifically denied that the First Respondent brought the Second Respondent into the business to inject some youth into the retail operation as alleged or at all. The Second Respondent was recruited because she was the best candidate for the role of area manager. The Claimant did not apply for the Second Respondent's role, probably as an acknowledgment that the Claimant would have been vastly underqualified.

The allegations against the Second Respondent

16. Paragraph 11 is denied. To the contrary, the Claimant made clear to the Second Respondent that she would not tolerate being managed by someone who was considerably younger than her, despite the Second Respondent's credentials and best efforts. Specifically, the Claimant was overheard at an after-work drinks event to welcome the Second Respondent in the evening of 25th September 2024 saying, "*It must be past her bedtime*".

17. Paragraph 12 is partly admitted. It is admitted that the Second Respondent attended the Clapham Store for the first time on 25th September 2024 and met the Claimant. It is admitted that the Second Respondent did a presentation to all staff at that store, just as she had done at the other stores of the First Respondent to include her vision for the future of the First Respondent's business. Before the Second Respondent's recruitment, the First Respondent had undertaken some market research concerning the change in demographics of its customers since 2020, and had discovered that the age of its customers had increased, and its younger customers in the 18-30 year age category had largely turned away from the First Respondent's brand since 2020. The First Respondent was keen to reverse this trend, and encourage the younger customers to return to the First Respondent. This aim had been included as a key performance indicator for the Second Respondent. On 25th September 2024, the Second Respondent had observed that old stock was still being sold on the shop floor of the Clapham Store, which undermined the First Respondent's brand as fashion-forward. It is admitted that she used the phrase "*It is out with the old and in the new*" in this context. It is denied that this was related to age as alleged or at all. It is also admitted that the Second Respondent said that the market research demonstrated that the customers in the younger age bracket considered the First Respondent brand "*old and tired*", again, it is denied that this was related to age. It is denied

that the Second Respondent said anything about reinvigoration with "*new Gen Z energy*", as alleged or at all.

18. In general, in relation to anything said or done by the Second Respondent on 25th September, it is specifically denied that it had the purpose or effect of violating the Claimant's dignity, and/or creating an intimidating, hostile, degrading, humiliating or offensive environment for her. The Claimant is required to prove that the conduct of the Second Respondent had the prescribed effect on her. In reality, the Claimant understood that the Second Respondent was simply referring to the market research, and setting out her vision for the brand. It is denied that the Claimant tried to sound enthusiastic about any changes proposed by the Second Respondent; she was the opposite. Her intransigence towards her new line manager was obvious from the first meeting.

19. Paragraph 13 is denied, except that it is admitted that the Second Respondent visited the Clapham Store on 15th October 2024. As the Claimant entered the store, the Claimant commented on the Second Respondent's outfit, referring to her dress as a "*rather bold choice for a Tuesday morning*". The Claimant then said of her own outfit words to the effect "*I feel like such a Granny in these trousers*". The Second Respondent did not say words to this effect at all, and did not respond directly to the Claimant's words.

20. Paragraph 14 is denied, except that it is admitted that there was an Area Sales meeting on 20th November 2024, attended by the Second Respondent and the Claimant, and, as Area Manager, the Second Respondent made several presentations. At no point did the Second Respondent, or anyone else to the knowledge of either Respondent, make the offensive comment attributed to the Second Respondent by the Claimant. It would make no commercial sense to dissuade any customers from browsing the stores, regardless of their age, and the Respondents would not have suggested anything of the sort.

21. Paragraph 15 is denied except that it is admitted that the Claimant's annual appraisal took place on 15th December 2024 with the Second Respondent. Specifically, it is denied that the Clapham Store had been the best performing store. Since the Claimant's arrival, sales had fallen in the store and it had become the worst performing store in the final quarter of 2024. It is denied that the staff turnover was low in comparison to the other stores of the First Respondent. It is not admitted that the Claimant's rating of Excellent was deserved in December 2023, but it is denied that such a high rating was deserved by the end of 2024.

22. Paragraph 16 is also denied except where admitted below. The Second Respondent appraised the Claimant's performance and conduct at work fairly and honestly. The First Respondent had received several reports of the Claimant's obstructive nature, repeated sniping about the Second Respondent's arrival and unwillingness to embrace the changes proposed by the Second Respondent. Sales figures had also decreased substantially, particularly in the last quarter of 2024. The Second Respondent has no recollection of saying that the Claimant was "*stuck in her ways*", or words to that effect, and it is denied that she said the Claimant had to keep up with her young staff, as alleged or at all. It is admitted that the Claimant was given a rating of "Below expectations" but it is asserted that the rating was a fair and reasonable one which was reflective of the Claimant's performance in 2024. It is admitted that the Claimant did not receive a bonus, but only those who received an "Excellent / Exceeding expectations" rating did receive such a bonus. It is admitted that Ms Cole, who was 32 years old at the time, received an "Excellent" rating because her performance was fairly appraised at that level. It is denied that the Notting Hill store did not perform as well as the Clapham Store.

The Instagram Bonus Scheme

23. In relation to paragraph 17, it is admitted that a new bonus scheme was announced on 1st February 2025, as described. The Respondent used the Instagram Bonus Scheme to boost marketing aimed at the younger demographic which had been dwindling in their customer base since 2020. The Claimant has omitted to mention the Instagram training offered to all staff, regardless of age which was offered throughout 2024 and into 2025. Many employees who had previously not had an Instagram account had been assisted to open an account and had, by February 2025, regardless of their age, amassed considerable followers. It is denied that the Claimant could not compete. Had the Claimant embraced social media, as many of her colleagues did, regardless of their age, as encouraged by the First Respondent, she may have won the bonus herself. Although in March 2025, those eligible for a bonus were all aged between 24 and 39 years, in April 2025 the age range of those successful was 33 to 52 years.

The application for the Flagship Store

24. In relation to paragraph 18, it is admitted that the management position for the Flagship Store was advertised in January 2025 with a starting salary of £50,000, and the Claimant applied on 14th January 2025. It is denied that the Claimant was the most experienced manager of any of the First Respondent's stores. It is admitted that the Claimant, on 20th February 2025, was interviewed by the Second Respondent. It is denied there was any hostility towards the Claimant and it is also denied that the Claimant interviewed well. In comparison to the majority of other candidates, it was clear on a fair assessment that the Claimant was not suitable for the role.

25. The first three sentences of paragraph 19 are admitted and the rest of the paragraph is denied. The entirety of the letter

informing the Claimant of her lack of success will be referred to in evidence, to demonstrate the context of the comments made therein. It is denied that Ms Hillier had little retail experience; she had spent the last three years successfully managing and increasing the profile of a smaller but very well-known brand's boutique in central London. It was hoped that Ms Hillier could emulate her success for the benefit of the First Respondent. Ms Hillier was objectively the better candidate for the role, which is why she was preferred. The decision to recruit Ms Hillier had nothing whatsoever to do with her age, and neither did the decision not to recruit the Claimant for the role.

26. In relation to paragraph 20, it is admitted that on 20th March 2025 the Claimant raised a grievance alleging age discrimination and harassment. These allegations were and are groundless. It is nevertheless admitted that the grievance constituted a protected act under s.27(2)(d) EqA. It is denied that the grievance was ignored. The Respondent acknowledged the grievance on 23rd March 2025 and had started the process of appointing an investigating officer before the Claimant resigned.

27. In relation to paragraph 21, since the Claimant was not at work on 25th March 2025, the Second Respondent did not have an opportunity to explain that new window merchandising was being put in place at every store. The Second Respondent was obliged to remove the old merchandising material and dress the windows in the same way as other stores were. It is denied that the Second Respondent uttered the words attributed to her by the Claimant, or any words to that effect. The Second Respondent's actions cannot accurately be described as "retaliation" at all; she was simply redressing the windows of the Clapham Store.

<u>The Claimant's resignation</u>

28. In relation to paragraphs 22 to 24, although the Claimant's alleged devastation is for her to prove, it is admitted that the Claimant next attended work on 28th March 2025 and she resigned with immediate effect on the same day, in breach of clause 4 of her contract of employment which required her to give three months' notice of termination. Discrimination, harassment, victimisation, constructive dismissal, and any breach of contract by the First Respondent are all denied.

<u>The defence to the claims</u>

<u>Harassment – s.26 EqA 2010</u>

29. In relation to paragraph 25:

    29.1 It is denied that the Second Respondent spoke about reinvigoration with "*new Gen Z energy*". It is admitted that the Second Respondent said "*It's out with the old, and in with the new!*"; and she also referred to criticism of the First Respondent's brand as being old and tired. In the context in which the words were said, they were not related to age, and did not violate the Claimant's dignity, and/or create an intimidating, hostile, degrading, humiliating or offensive environment for the Claimant.

    29.2 It is denied that the Second Respondent said any words to the effect of "*Oh my God, Jackie, you look like such a Granny in that outfit!*" on 15th October 2024 as alleged or at all.

    29.3 It is denied that the First or Second Respondents on the 20th November 2024 or at all issued instructions to dissuade older customers from browsing the stores, and it is also denied that the Second Respondent said "*We don't want a load of geriatrics damaging the brand*" as alleged or at all.

29.4 It is not admitted that the Second Respondent said, on 15th December 2024 or at all, that the Claimant was "*stuck in your ways*"; and it is denied that the Second Respondent said the Claimant had to keep up with her young staff. It is admitted that on or around 15th December 2024, the Second Respondent discussed with the Claimant, at her appraisal, reports of the Claimant's obstructive nature, repeated sniping about the Second Respondent's arrival and unwillingness to embrace the changes proposed by the Second Respondent. It is denied that these discussions related to age in any way. It is also denied that the appraisal discussion violated the Claimant's dignity, and/or created an intimidating, hostile, degrading, humiliating or offensive environment for the Claimant.

29.5 It is admitted that the 18th March 2025 letter stated that the Claimant lacked the "*dynamism*" the First Respondent was looking for to respond to "*rapidly changing times*". It is denied that the letter, or any part of it, related to age in any way. It is also denied that the letter violated the Claimant's dignity, and/or created an intimidating, hostile, degrading, humiliating or offensive environment for the Claimant.

It is denied that the Second Respondent harassed the Claimant related to age, contrary to s.26 EqA, as alleged or at all.

Direct age discrimination

30. In relation to paragraph 26:

30.1 It is admitted that the Claimant's performance was rated as "Below expectations" on or around 15th December 2024. It is denied that the Claimant deserved any higher score on any objective assessment. It is denied that age had anything to do with the Claimant's performance rating. It is denied that a hypothetical comparator of a younger age would have been treated more favourably than the Claimant. A hypothetical comparator with the same performance record as the Claimant would have been given the same performance rating. Ms Cole is not an appropriate statutory comparator, under s.23 EqA, because her circumstances, including her performance as a store manager, were materially different to the Claimant's.

30.2 By not being paid a Christmas bonus of £500, the Claimant was treated in the same way as every employee, regardless of their age, who did not achieve a rating of "Excellent / Exceeding Expectations" in their appraisal. It is denied that the decision not to pay the Claimant a Christmas bonus had anything to do with age. It is denied that a hypothetical comparator of a younger age would have been paid the Christmas bonus. A hypothetical comparator with the same performance rating as the Claimant would not have been paid the bonus. Ms Cole is not an appropriate statutory comparator, under s.23 EqA, because her circumstances, including her performance rating, were materially different to the Claimant's.

30.3 It is admitted that the Claimant was not appointed to manage the Flagship Store. It is denied that this decision had anything to do with her age. It is also denied that a hypothetical comparator of a younger age would have been treated more favourably than the Claimant. A hypothetical comparator with the same application (including interview performance) as the Claimant would not have been appointed to the role. Ms Hillier is not an appropriate statutory comparator, under s.23 EqA, because her circumstances, including her application and interview performance, were materially different to the Claimant's.

30.4 It is denied that the Claimant was constructively dismissed as alleged or at all.

31. It is denied that the Claimant was directly discriminated against because of her age, contrary to s.13 EqA, as alleged or at all.

<u>Indirect discrimination – s.19 EqA</u>

32. Paragraph 28 is denied except that it is admitted that the Instagram Bonus Scheme was a provision, criterion or practice which was applied to all employees of all ages. It is denied that it placed, or would place, older employees of over the age of 40 years at a particular disadvantage. Older employees of the First Respondent were not less likely than the employees under 35 years, to have an Instagram account, because the First Respondent had provided all employees with training on how to open an account. The introduction of the Instagram Bonus Scheme did not put the Claimant at a disadvantage in comparison to her younger colleagues. In the alternative, even if the PCP was disadvantageous to younger employees and the Claimant, the First Respondent can show that it was a proportionate means of achieving a legitimate aim, that is effectively and efficiently to market the First Respondent's brand to the First Respondent's target audience; to improve the corporate image of the brand.

33. It is denied that the Claimant was indirectly discriminated against by the First Respondent, contrary to s.19 EqA, as alleged or at all.

Victimisation – s.27 EqA

34. Paragraph 29 is denied except that it is admitted that the Claimant did a protected act, as defined by s.27(2)(d) EqA by raising a grievance on 20th March 2025. It is denied that the Second Respondent destroyed the Claimant's window merchandising on 25th March 2025, she simply removed it because it was due to be replaced to replicate the windows of the First Respondent's other stores. It is denied that the change of window dressing on 25th March 2025 was caused in any way by the Claimant's protected act, or because it was believed that the Claimant had done a protected act.

35. It is therefore denied that the Claimant was victimised, contrary to s.27 EqA, as alleged or at all.

Disposal of claims

36. In relation to paragraphs 30 to 32, it is denied that the Claimant is entitled to any of the compensation or relief claimed because her claims should be dismissed.

37. Alternatively, and in any event, it is likely that the Claimant's employment would have come to an end in any event within a relatively short time, and likely, before she acquired statutory rights in June 2025, due to her poor performance in her role as manager of the Clapham Store and/or her obstructive misconduct towards the Second Respondent. If, contrary to the defence set out above, any claims are upheld, the Tribunal will be invited to reflect the fact that a lawful termination was inevitable in any compensation awarded on a just and equitable basis.

38. Retail store managers are very much in demand and the Claimant has failed to take reasonable steps to mitigate her loss because she

has not secured alternative employment at comparable remuneration within one to two months of her resignation.

39. It is also denied that there was any breach of the ACAS Code of Practice on Disciplinary and Grievance Procedures on the First Respondent's part. The Claimant's grievance was not ignored. The First Respondent acknowledged and started the process of appointing an investigator before the Claimant resigned. At the point of resignation, the Claimant was no longer an employee and the ACAS Code no longer applied. To the contrary, the Claimant unreasonably failed to set out all of her complaints in her grievance and resigned before the grievance process could be completed. Any compensation found to be payable to her should be reduced by up to 25%, pursuant to s.207A Trade Union and Labour Relations (Consolidation) Act 1992.

40. The claims should be dismissed, if not struck out for want of jurisdiction.

[NAME OF RESPONDENT OR REPRESENTATIVE]

[DATE]

APPENDIX C

All names are fictional and the factual information is imagined. Any resemblance to any real people or events is entirely coincidental.

IN THE [CENTRAL LONDON] EMPLOYMENT TRIBUNAL

Case no.: 1231234/2025

B E T W E E N :

Ms JACQUELINE SMITH

Claimant

-and-

MGKMRT LTD

First Respondent

Ms NINA BLACK

Second Respondent

DRAFT / AGREED LIST OF ISSUES

FOR CONSIDERATION AT THE PRELIMINARY HEARING ON [DATE]

Harassment – s.26 EqA

1. Did the Second Respondent say and do the following:

   1.1 on 25th September 2024: "*It's out with the old, and in with the new!*"; criticising the First Respondent brand for being old and tired; referring to needing reinvigoration with "*new Gen Z energy*";

   1.2 on 15th October 2024, "*Oh my God, Jackie, you look like such a Granny in that outfit!*";

   1.3 on the 20th November 2024 instructions to dissuade older customers from browsing the stores and saying "*We don't want a load of geriatrics damaging the brand*";

   1.4 on 15th December 2024 saying the Claimant was too slow to accept change, was obstructive and difficult to work with; "*stuck in your ways*" and she had to keep up with her young staff;

   1.5 the 18th March 2025 letter stating the Claimant lacked the "*dynamism*" the First Respondent was looking for to respond to "*rapidly changing times*"?

2. Was this conduct unwanted by the Claimant?

3. Did this conduct relate to age?

4. Did the conduct have the purpose or effect of violating the Claimant's dignity, and/or creating an intimidating, hostile, degrading, humiliating or offensive environment for the Claimant?

Direct age discrimination – s.13 EqA

5. Was the Claimant was treated in the following ways by the First and/or Second Respondent:

   5.1 given an appraisal rating of "Below expectations" on 15th December 2024, rather than the "Excellent" rating which she deserved, contrary to the treatment of a hypothetical comparator under the age of 35 years, or of Elise Cole;

   5.2 not being paid the £500 Christmas bonus, contrary to the treatment of a hypothetical comparator under the age of 35 years, or of Elise Cole;

   5.3 not being appointed the manager of the Flagship Store, contrary to the treatment of a hypothetical comparator under the age of 35 years, or of Marcia Hillier;

   5.4 constructively dismissed on 28th March 2025?

6. Was the Claimant's treatment because she was over the age of 40 years?

7. Was the Claimant's treatment less favourable treatment than a hypothetical person under the age of 35 years, or the actual comparators named above (Elise Cole and Marcia Hillier)?

8. Was the Claimant's treatment a proportionate means of achieving a legitimate aim? [*Respondent to confirm at the preliminary hearing whether or not a justification defence is being pursued in respect of the direct age discrimination claim*].

Indirect age discrimination – s.19 EqA

9. Did the First Respondent's Instagram Bonus Scheme constitute a provision, criterion or practice which was applied to all employees of all ages? [*Admitted by the Respondents*].

10. Did the Instagram Bonus Scheme place, or would place, older employees of over the age of 40 years at a particular disadvantage because the older employees were less likely than the employees under 35 years, to have an Instagram account, established or at all?

11. Did the Instagram Bonus Scheme put the Claimant at a disadvantage in comparison to her younger colleagues (under the age of 35 years)?

12. Can the First Respondent show that the PCP was a means of achieving the following aims:

    12.1 effectively and efficiently to market the First Respondent's brand to the First Respondent's target audience;

    12.2 to improve the corporate image of the brand?

13. Were those aims legitimate? [*Admitted by the Claimant*].

14. Were the means to achieve them proportionate?

Victimisation – s.27 EqA

15. Did the Claimant do a protected act, as defined by s.27(2)(d) EqA by raising a grievance on 20th March 2025? [*The Respondents admit the protected act*].

16. Did the Second Respondent destroy the Claimant's window merchandising on 25th March 2025?

17. If so, did the Second Respondent do that because of the Claimant's protected act, or because she believed the Claimant had done or may do a protected act?

Liability of Respondents

18. Is the First Respondent liable under ss.39-40 EqA, for any discriminatory acts upheld as the Claimant's employer? [*The First Respondent admits this*].

19. Is the Second Respondent liable under s.110(1) EqA for any discriminatory acts upheld?

20. Was the Second Respondent in the course of her employment at the time discriminatory acts are alleged?

21. If so, is the First Respondent liable for the discriminatory actions of the Second Respondent pursuant to s.109(1) EqA? [*The First Respondent admits this if paragraph 20 is answered affirmatively and confirms that it is not seeking to rely upon the statutory defence in s.109(4) EqA in respect of the Second Respondent's actions or omissions*].

Limitation – s.123 EqA

22. On what dates did the alleged discriminatory acts / omissions / course of conduct happen?

23. Were any of the Claimant's claims were presented outside of the primary time limit set out at s.123 EqA (not including the ACAS EC period and bearing in mind any extension to the time limit)? [*The parties are agreed that: the Claimant began ACAS Early Conciliation on 2nd June 2025 and the certificate was issued on 10th June 2025. The Claimant presented her claims on 27th June 2025. Any claim complaining of events which took place on or before the 2nd March 2025 is prima facie out of time*]?

24. If so, is it just and equitable to extend time to allow the claims to proceed?

Remedy – ss.119, 124 EqA, s.207A TULRCA

25. If the claims succeed, is the Claimant entitled to a Declaration that she has been discriminated against within the meaning of s.124(2)(a) EqA?

26. If the claims succeed, is the Claimant entitled to a Recommendation pursuant to s.124(2)(c) EqA? [*The Claimant is asked to clarify what Recommendations she would be pursuing*].

27. If the claims succeed what is the just and equitable level of compensation to be awarded considering:

    27.1 Alleged loss of bonus of £500 in Christmas 2024;

    27.2 Alleged loss of bonus from the Instagram Bonus Scheme from 1st March 2025;

    27.3 Alleged loss of payrise (to £50,000 pa) associated with a promotion in or around March 2025;

    27.4 Alleged loss of earnings flowing from the termination of her employment, including future loss;

    27.5 Alleged injury to feelings;

    27.6 Interest;

    27.7 Has the Claimant taken reasonable steps to mitigate her loss?

    27.8 If not, what loss of earnings would have been incurred if she had taken reasonable steps to mitigate her loss?

    27.9 The extent to which the lawful termination of the Claimant's employment and/or the lawful denial of bonuses / a payrise was inevitable or likely?

28. Did either party fail to follow the ACAS Code of Practice on Disciplinary and Grievance Procedures in respect of the Claimant's grievance dated the 20th March 2025? [*Both Claimant and First Respondent to specify at preliminary hearing what paragraphs of the ACAS CoP was allegedly breached*].

29. Is either an uplift or reduction of up to 25% in any compensation found to be payable, just and equitable, pursuant to s.207A Trade Union and Labour Relations (Consolidation) Act 1992?

INDEX

MORE BOOKS BY LAW BRIEF PUBLISHING

'The Electronic Communications Code: A Practical Guide – Second Edition' by Kerry Bretherton KC, James Castle, Mark Loveday
'A Practical Guide to the Independent School Standards – September 2023 Edition' by Sarah McKimm
'A Practical Guide to Estate Administration and Crypto Assets' by Richard Marshall
'A Practical Guide to Parental Alienation in Private and Public Law Children Cases' by Sam King QC & Frankie Shama
'Contested Heritage – Removing Art from Land and Historic Buildings' by Richard Harwood QC, Catherine Dobson, David Sawtell
'The Limits of Separate Legal Personality: When Those Running a Company Can Be Held Personally Liable for Losses Caused to Third Parties Outside of the Company' by Dr Mike Wilkinson
'A Practical Guide to Transgender Law' by Robin Moira White & Nicola Newbegin
'A Practical Guide to 'Stranded Spouses' in Family Law' by Mani Singh Basi
'A Practical Guide to Residential Freehold Conveyancing' by Lorraine Richardson
'A Practical Guide to Pensions on Divorce for Lawyers' by Bryan Scant
'A Practical Guide to Challenging Sham Marriage Allegations in Immigration Law' by Priya Solanki
'A Practical Guide to Digital Communications Evidence in Criminal Law' by Sam Willis
'A Practical Guide to Legal Rights in Scotland' by Sarah-Jane Macdonald
'A Practical Guide to New Build Conveyancing' by Paul Sams & Rebecca East
'A Practical Guide to Inherited Wealth on Divorce' by Hayley Trim
'A Practical Guide to Practice Direction 12J and Domestic Abuse in Private Law Children Proceedings' by Rebecca Cross & Malvika Jaganmohan
'A Practical Guide to Confiscation and Restraint' by Narita Bahra QC, John Carl Townsend, David Winch
'A Practical Guide to the Law of Forests in Scotland' by Philip Buchan
'A Practical Guide to Health and Medical Cases in Immigration Law' by Rebecca Chapman & Miranda Butler
'A Practical Guide to Bad Character Evidence for Criminal Practitioners by Aparna Rao
'A Practical Guide to Extradition Law post-Brexit' by Myles Grandison et al
'A Practical Guide to Hoarding and Mental Health for Housing Lawyers' by Rachel Coyle

'Stephens on Contractual Indemnities' by Richard Stephens
'A Practical Guide to the EU Succession Regulation' by Richard Frimston
'A Practical Guide to Solicitor and Client Costs – Second Edition' by Robin Dunne
'Constructive Dismissal – Practice Pointers and Principles' by Benjimin Burgher
'A Practical Guide to Religion and Belief Discrimination Claims in the Workplace' by Kashif Ali
'A Practical Guide to the Law of Medical Treatment Decisions' by Ben Troke
'Fundamental Dishonesty and QOCS in Personal Injury Proceedings: Law and Practice' by Jake Rowley
'A Practical Guide to the Law in Relation to School Exclusions' by Charlotte Hadfield & Alice de Coverley
'A Practical Guide to Divorce for the Silver Separators' by Karin Walker
'The Right to be Forgotten – The Law and Practical Issues' by Melissa Stock
'A Practical Guide to Planning Law and Rights of Way in National Parks, the Broads and AONBs' by James Maurici QC, James Neill et al
'A Practical Guide to Election Law' by Tom Tabori
'A Practical Guide to the Law in Relation to Surrogacy' by Andrew Powell
'A Practical Guide to Claims Arising from Fatal Accidents – Second Edition' by James Patience
'A Practical Guide to Asbestos Claims' by Jonathan Owen & Gareth McAloon
'A Practical Guide to Stamp Duty Land Tax in England and Northern Ireland' by Suzanne O'Hara
'A Practical Guide to the Law of Farming Partnerships' by Philip Whitcomb
'A Practical Guide to the Law of Unlawful Eviction and Harassment – Second Edition' by Stephanie Lovegrove
'A Practical Guide to Costs in Personal Injury Claims – Second Edition' by Matthew Hoe
'A Practical Guide to the General Data Protection Regulation (GDPR) – Second Edition' by Keith Markham
'A Practical Guide to Working with Litigants in Person and McKenzie Friends in Family Cases' by Stuart Barlow
'Protecting Unregistered Brands: A Practical Guide to the Law of Passing Off' by Lorna Brazell
'A Practical Guide to Secondary Liability and Joint Enterprise Post-Jogee' by Joanne Cecil & James Mehigan

'A Practical Guide to the Pre-Action RTA Claims Protocol for Personal Injury Lawyers' by Antonia Ford
'A Practical Guide to Neighbour Disputes and the Law' by Alexander Walsh
'A Practical Guide to Coercive Control for Legal Practitioners and Victims' by Rachel Horman
'A Practical Guide to the Law of Driverless Cars – Second Edition'
by Alex Glassbrook, Emma Northey & Scarlett Milligan
'A Practical Guide to TOLATA Claims' by Greg Williams
'A Practical Guide to Elderly Law – Second Edition' by Justin Patten
'A Practical Guide to Responding to Housing Disrepair and Unfitness Claims' by Iain Wightwick
'A Practical Guide to the Law of Bullying and Harassment in the Workplace' by Philip Hyland
'How to Be a Freelance Solicitor: A Practical Guide to the SRA-Regulated Freelance Solicitor Model' by Paul Bennett
'A Practical Guide to Prison Injury Claims' by Malcolm Johnson
'A Practical Guide to Advising Clients at the Police Station' by Colin Stephen McKeown-Beaumont
'A Practical Guide to Antisocial Behaviour Injunctions – Second Edition' by Iain Wightwick
'Practical Mediation: A Guide for Mediators, Advocates, Advisers, Lawyers, and Students in Civil, Commercial, Business, Property, Workplace, and Employment Cases' by Jonathan Dingle with John Sephton
'The Mini-Pupillage Workbook' by David Boyle
'A Practical Guide to Crofting Law' by Brian Inkster
'A Practical Guide to the Law of Domain Names and Cybersquatting' by Andrew Clemson
'A Practical Guide to the Law of Gender Pay Gap Reporting' by Harini Iyengar
'NHS Whistleblowing and the Law' by Joseph England
'Employment Law and the Gig Economy' by Nigel Mackay & Annie Powell
'A Practical Guide to Noise Induced Hearing Loss (NIHL) Claims' by Andrew Mckie, Ian Skeate, Gareth McAloon
'An Introduction to Beauty Negligence Claims – A Practical Guide for the Personal Injury Practitioner' by Greg Almond
'Intercompany Agreements for Transfer Pricing Compliance' by Paul Sutton
'Zen and the Art of Mediation' by Martin Plowman
'A Practical Guide to Adoption for Family Lawyers' by Graham Pegg

www.ingramcontent.com/pod-product-compliance
Ingram Content Group UK Ltd.
Pitfield, Milton Keynes, MK11 3LW, UK
UKHW020136290926
15471UKWH00003B/514

9 781916 698017